SELF-CATERING IN FRANCE

OTHER SELF-CATERING GUIDES PUBLISHED BY CROOM HELM

Self-catering in Portugal
Carol Wright

Self-catering in Greece, Mainland and Islands
Florica Kyriacopoulos and Tim Salmon

Self-catering in Spain
Carole Stewart with Chris Stewart

Self-catering in Italy
Susan Grossman

Self-catering Afloat
Bill Glenton

SELF-CATERING IN FRANCE

Making the most of local food and drink

Arthur and Barbara Eperon

CHRISTOPHER HELM
London

Line drawings by Mike Dodd
Christopher Helm (Publishers) Ltd, Imperial House,
21-25 North Street, Bromley, Kent BR1 1SD

British Library Cataloguing in Publication Data

Eperon, Arthur
Self-catering in France : making the most
of local food and drink.
1. Cookery, French 2. Beverages — France
I. Title II. Eperon, Barbara
641′.0944 TX719

ISBN 0-7470-0801-9

Typeset by Leaper and Gard Ltd, Bristol
Printed and bound in the Channel Islands by
The Guernsey Press Co. Ltd, Channel Islands

Contents

Regional Map

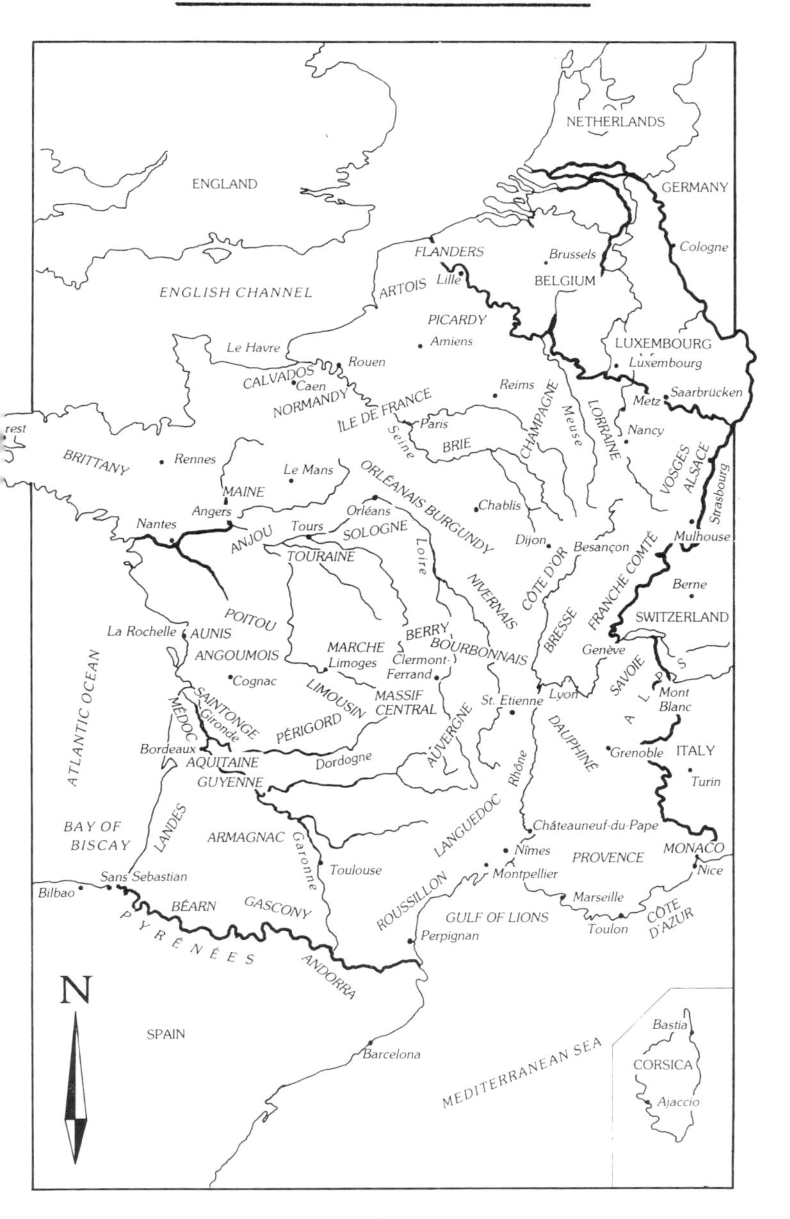

1

BUYING FOOD

The temptation on a self-catering holiday in France is to do very little catering for yourself at all, unless, of course, you have young children with you. Many small town and country restaurants still offer good meals for half the price of elsewhere, so the temptation is to picnic at lunchtime on French bread and a local pâté or cheese with tomatoes, then dine in a little restaurant to leave maximum time for sightseeing, beach-lounging or just resting.

Then you visit a local market and the desire to cater and cook comes flooding back as you see farm cheeses and slabs of local butter, freshly made pâtés in bowls and terrines, piles of colourful fresh fruits and delicious seasonal fresh vegetables like mange-tout peas, little green spring broad beans and tiny thin green string beans, crisp white cauliflowers, luscious field tomatoes (which make you dream of tomato salad), plump radishes and young orange and white carrots, with herbs in live sprigs or dried in little sacks to be weighed out to your wishes. There will be succulent, tempting joints of meat, like shoulder of lamb off the bone and rolled ready for stuffing; and 0.5m long rolls of topside or sirloin, perhaps a fish stall with mounds of oysters, mussels and prawns alongside salmon, trout, sole and red mullet along with strange shiny fishes we cannot identify.

The secret is to avoid rigidity in cooking or eating out, to let the weather, the sights you want to see and your own whims and fancies decide for you. Unless you want to follow a special recipe, don't go shopping with a set meal in mind — buy and cook *à marché* (according to the market) as the French do, buying the freshest, best-value items first, then the other items you need to cook or eat with them. Keep in store some cold meat, sausages (including one that needs cooking), eggs, cheese, pâté in case you change plans. If you don't need them they can be used for a picnic lunch.

When you arrive at your accommodation, whether it is a remote cottage, town flat or tent or caravan on a site with a shop and restaurant, find out first the place and day of the week of any markets within reasonable distance and the names of two good cheap restaurants. If the person who hands over the keys to you cannot tell you, ask at the post office, the local bar (*outside* a camping site) and the baker's shop (*boulangerie*) where you buy your first loaf of bread. Ask all of them. Then find out the best of the local shops and their opening hours. Most small food shops open around 8.00 to 8.30 a.m. close for lunch from 12.00 to 2.00 p.m. or 2.30 p.m. and are open again until about 7.00 p.m., but these hours vary with seasons and areas.

SHOPS

Boucherie The butcher. They used to sell beef, veal and lamb but now also sell pork. Lamb is a luxury in France. Pork is cheapest. They sell raw bacon and even ham and most sell poultry and game. They also sell plastic containers of cooking fats, too – lard (pork fat – what we call 'lard' is *saindoux*), *graisse d'oie* (goose fat), *graisse de rognon* (suet).

Boucherie Chevaline Sells horsemeat (usually has a horse's head sign outside).

Boulangerie The baker's shop. Bread is baked on the spot. The baker usually makes *croissants*, *brioches* and some plainer cakes. Most visitors (and the French themselves) buy long white loaves (*baguettes*) but health and fibre followers will be glad to know that many bakers now sell wholemeal bread (*pain intégral* or *complet*); though a few bakers buy this from a bread factory, as they do rye bread (*pain de seigle*). Arthur likes the rough, long-keeping, fairly hard country bread (*pain de campagne*), often in a round loaf. Ask for it and try it. If you are unlucky and there is no boulangerie in your village, you may have to buy at the grocer (*épicerie*) or at the supermarket where the bread is likely to have been delivered from a factory.

If you cannot get to a baker every morning before breakfast, buy extra *croissants* one morning and put them in a plastic bag in the freezer compartment or ice tray of the fridge. They will keep several days. Heat them under the grill. Not quite as nice as fresh, they are better than cold, double baked or factory *croissant*.

Charcuterie Originally a pork butcher's shop, selling pork raw, cooked, cured, dried and smoked, in sausages, terrines and pâtés. Now most sell prepared meat dishes, too, pies, savoury flans (such as *quiche Lorraine*), even casseroles or curries, plus mayonnaise salads. Neither these dishes nor the take-aways from the pastry shops (*pâtisseries*) are what health or food faddists call 'junk food'. They are fresh-cooked and prepared on the premises. Coarser sausages and pâtés are usually milder than smooth varieties. In France you can ask to taste pâtés and cheeses.

Confiserie Confectioners, mostly absorbed these days by the pâtisseries but still around in big towns and areas where thev specialise in making chocolates or other sweets. These are often made on the spot and can be superb but very expensive.

Epicerie (also Alimentation) Grocers. The old style grocer has almost died out, replaced by self-service shops where everything except, perhaps, fruit and vegetables are pre-packed, delivered from a wholesaler. Many are referred to as 'Le Self' and have little identity. In the country, though, they may well sell local vegetables, fruit, cheese, poultry and game. Supermarkets will almost invariably sell only factory cheese, kept refrigerated, which is all right for some cheeses but the death of others, such as Camembert and many blue cheeses.

Fromagerie Cheese shop found these days, alas, only in a few cities. Inevitably, they are smelly, an aroma Arthur loves. Barbara prefers the smell of the boulangerie. Anyway, don't buy cheeses without smell – they will have no taste. *Fromageries* do have *fermier* (farm-made) cheeses which are better because the milk is not pasteurised, which spoils the flavour.

Pâtisserie Cake shop, selling also ice cream and sorbet, and sometimes thick fresh cream from a bowl. The pâtisserie ranges from *profiteroles* (like éclairs) and other concoctions oozing cream to tarts and flans filled with fruit or conserve. Those French housewives who can afford to buy a lot of their desserts here. Some pâtisseries sell savoury dishes which you can also buy at the charcuterie, such as *quiche Lorraine* (flan of pastry filled with bacon, eggs and cream) and *bouchée à la reine* (*vol au vent* filled with creamy chicken mixture), but often they cost more here.

Poissonerie Fishmonger. A huge range of fish is available in France but obviously you cannot find a shop which stocks them all fresh, even in Paris. Watch for other fish items like fish soup in cans or even made especially for the shop and sold in jars, cans of *quenelles de brochet* (little light mousses made with pike), Nantua sauce to serve with *quenelles* or other fish (sauce of crayfish and cream), cans of *rouille* (hot sauce with peppers and saffron for fish), fish pâté (some are excellent), *hareng blanc* (salt herring), *fumé* (smoked herring), *saur* (salted and smoked). Smoked salmon, which usually comes from Norway, is regarded as the best in the world by the French though some visitors may find it undersmoked.

Traiteur The 'take-away' for everything from casseroles to pâtés, cooked meats, smoked meats and fish, salads of many sorts, but the name 'traiteur' is rarely used these days — they are given personalised names to raise their image. Very useful, much dearer since they turned 'snob', with a tendency to sell overpriced 'health' products and fashionably-named canned or boxed products where you pay double for the label. But local shops are not like that in small provincial towns.

With the young, the take-away and the fast food restaurant selling factory-produced hamburgers and pizzas are fashionable — temporarily, we hope.

Volailler The poulterer, selling also game and pâtés, terrines and cans of *confit* of duck and goose, and canned game.

Supermarché Often called 'Super' though some are just little local self-service grocers; others belong to national chains and they are especially useful for such things as detergents, seasoning, dish-cloths and brushes, branded goods like coffee, tea bags, sugar, salt, pepper and for items needed in a hurry or forgotton when shopping elsewhere. They are cheaper than individual shops. But it would be a pity to shop in them if you want to try any regional foods or dishes because most get their products from national wholesalers. Their cheese is especially dull. They may have a good choice of vegetables because they import them from all over France and abroad but they are often dearer than in the local grocer and nearly always less fresh. Their pâtés, too, are very 'factory'.

Hypermarché Hypermarkets ('cities' of shops) do vary but we like those which have individual shops, usually at the entrance, selling fish, wine or meat. These are nearly always branches of local shops.

SHOPPING

Where there are fishing boats, the fish markets are excellent. Boulogne's market alongside the fish dock, for instance, is very good when the boats can get to sea, but you must be there early in the morning. Roll up about 11.00 a.m. and you get what is left, at noon they are shutting down. Remember that some shellfish are usually sold raw in France, for example *langoustines*. Ask for fish heads to make a fish stock (*fumet*) for sauces.

French meat cuts vary a little from ours. See diagram for beef, lamb and pork.

You will see all sorts of foods, from beef, sausages and chickens to cheese, olives and vegetables (even potatoes) flaunting a red label with all sorts of information on the back – 'Le Label Rouge'. These products have the backing of the law. They must obey rigorous standards in the way they are produced, such as feed for chickens and breeds and place of origin for beef. They are a good guide to excellence but few products qualify and you will pay more for them.

WHAT TO READ?

We intended to include a dictionary of French food and drink words and terms. We found that there are so many you might want to know that it would have doubled the size of this book (and the price!).

The best book we know is *The Taste of France* (Macmillan) edited by Fay Sharman, but it is *not* pocket-sized and has only a French into English section. *What's on the Menu* (Atkinson) by Dr David Atkinson is not so extensive but is pocket-size, has a fairly good French into English section and a useful English into French word list (but without the 'le', 'la' genders of nouns).

WHAT TO BUY?

Advice on what to take home is difficult these days. The choice is very personal, and depends so much on what you have already; most French products are, of course, obtainable in our own cities, so often it is nowadays a matter of

VEAL

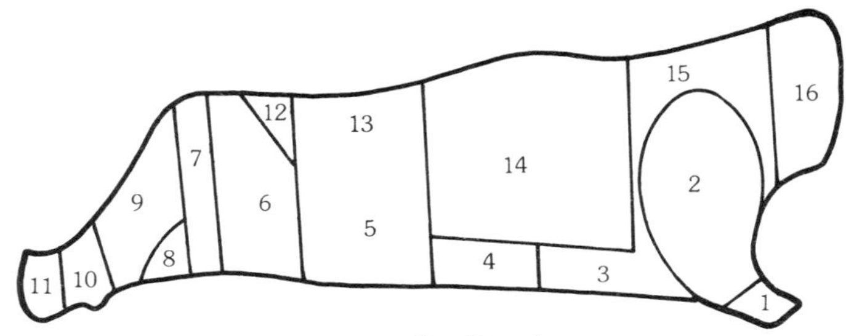

French

1 Jarret
2 Épaule
3 Poitrine
4 Tendron
5 Longe et rognon
6 Quasi or cul
7 Escalope
8 Fricandeau
9 Noix or ciuseau; grenadins
10 Jarret
11 Crosse
12 Nois patissière or fricandeau or sous-noix
13 Selle; filet
14 Côtelettes; carré
15 Côtelettes decouvertes
16 Collet

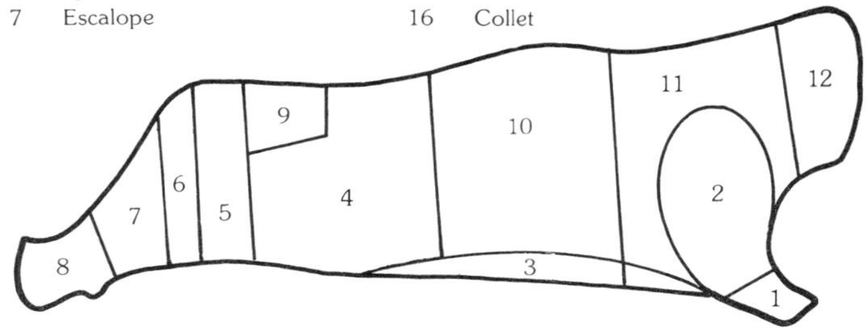

British

1 Knuckle
2 Shoulder
3 Breast
4 Loin, loin cutlets or saddle
5 Escalope, fillets or fillet roast
6 Escalope
7 Leg
8 Knuckle
9 Rump
10 Best end of neck cutlets or roast
11 Middle cutlets
12 Scrag end

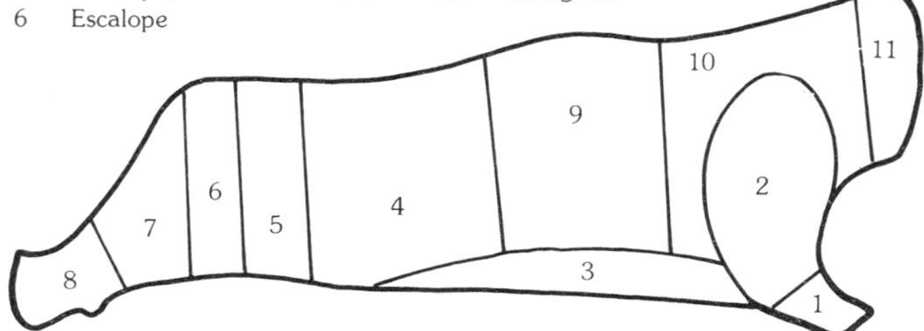

American

1 Shank
2 Shoulder
3 Breast
4 Loin roast, chops, steak
5 Rump roast
6 Steaks or scallops
7 Leg
8 Knuckle
9 Rib chops or rib roast
10 Shoulder chops
11 City chicken

LAMB

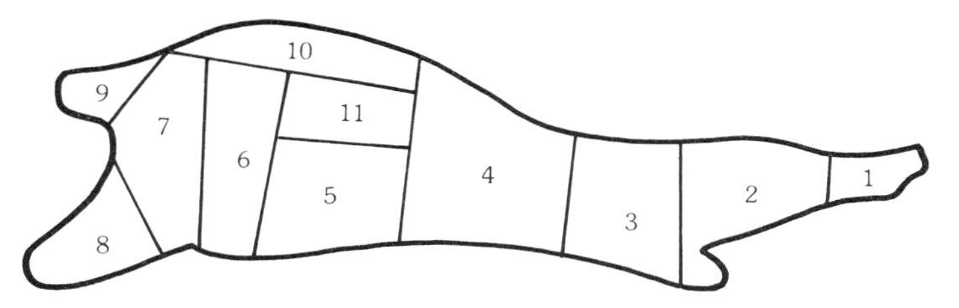

French

1 Pied
2 Gigot
3 Selle (saddle)
4 Filet and côte de filet
5 Côtes or côtelettes
6 Carré and côtes or côtelettes
6 and 7 (together) Épaule (shoulder)
8 Collet
9 Pied
10 Poitrine
11 Haute de côtelette

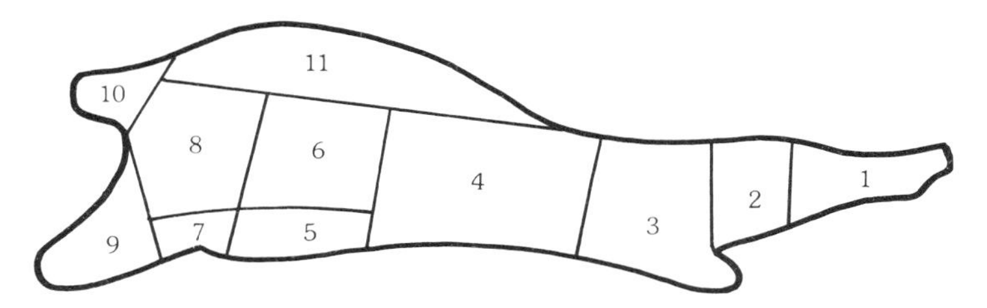

British

1 Shank
2 Leg
3 Fillet
4 Loin or centreloin chops (saddle)
5 Best end of neck
6 Cutlets
7 Chops/cutlets
7, 8 Shoulder
9 Scrag end/neck
10 Shank
11 Breast

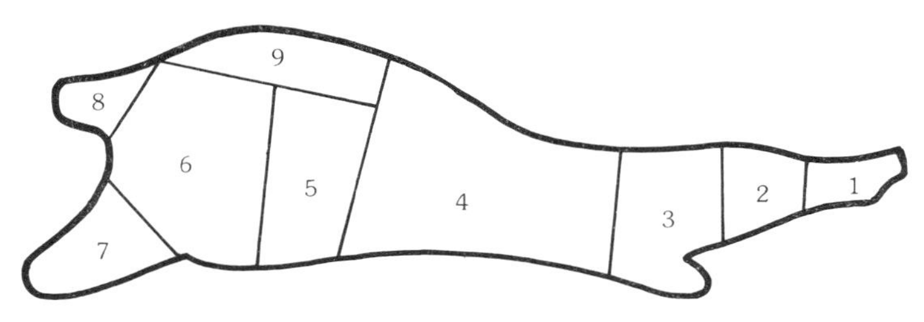

American

1 Shank
2 Leg steaks
2, 3 Gigot
4 Centreloin chops (saddle)
5 Rib chops or cut whole rack or crown roast
6 Shoulder
7 Neck
8 Shank
9 Breast

PORK

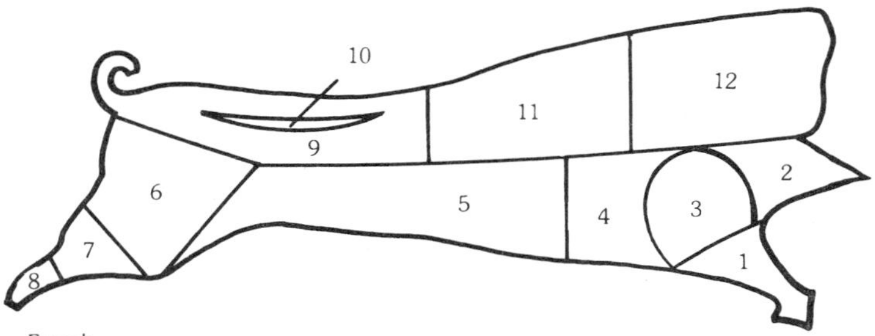

French

1 Pied
2 Gorge
3 Épaule or jambonneau
4 Plat de côtes
5 Poitrine
6 Jambon
9 Pointe de filet
10 Filet
11 Côtes (whole) and carré
12 Palette

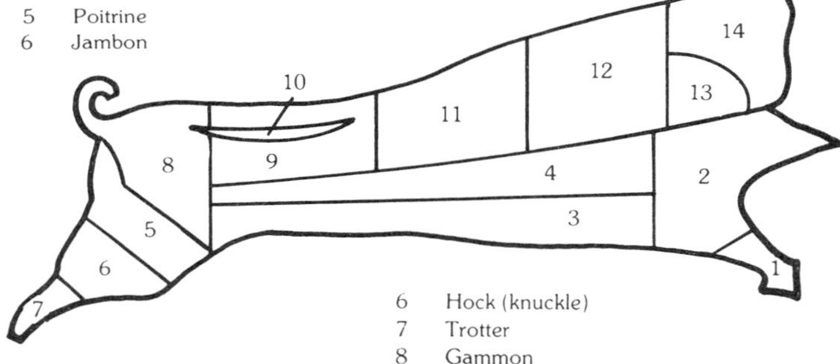

British

1 Trotter
2 Hand
3 Belly
4 Streaky bacon
5 Gammon slices
6 Hock (knuckle)
7 Trotter
8 Gammon
9 Chump and loin chops or hind loin joint
10 Fillet
11 Loin chops or fore loin roast
12 Shoulder cutlets
13 Blade bone
14 Spare ribs

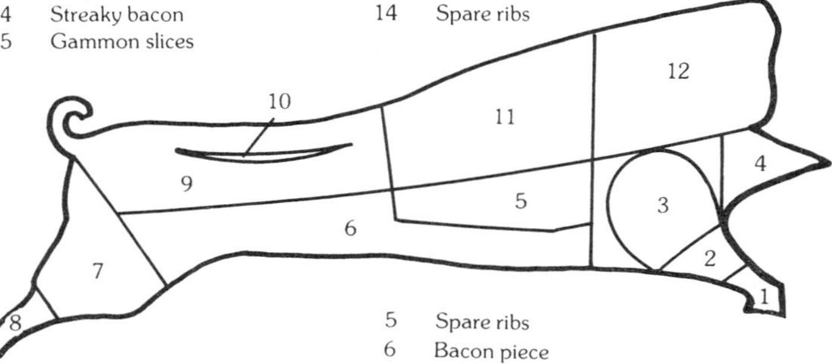

American

1 Foot
2 Hock
3 Shoulder
4 Jowl butt
5 Spare ribs
6 Bacon piece
7 Ham
8 Shank
9 Loin roast
10 Tenderloin
11 Loin chops or roast
12 Shoulder butt

BEEF

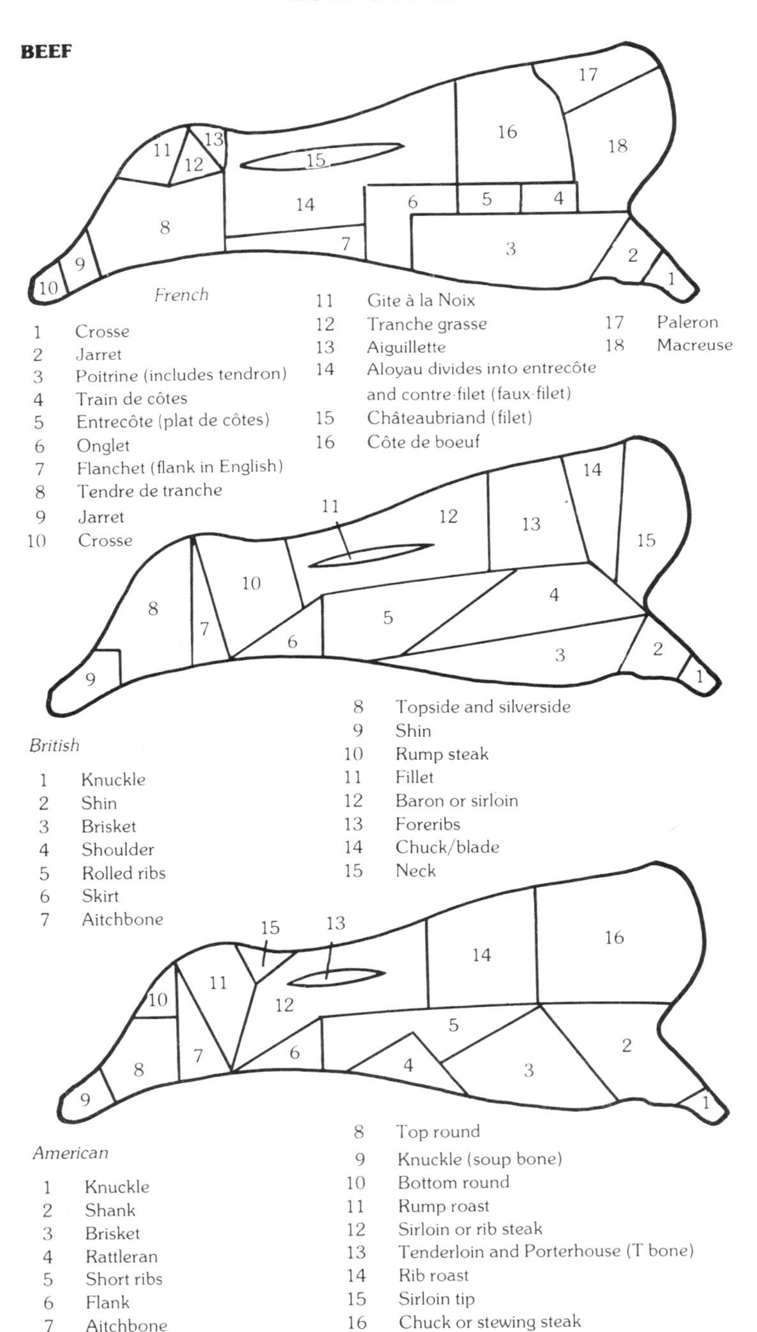

French

1 Crosse
2 Jarret
3 Poitrine (includes tendron)
4 Train de côtes
5 Entrecôte (plat de côtes)
6 Onglet
7 Flanchet (flank in English)
8 Tendre de tranche
9 Jarret
10 Crosse
11 Gite à la Noix
12 Tranche grasse
13 Aiguillette
14 Aloyau divides into entrecôte and contre-filet (faux-filet)
15 Châteaubriand (filet)
16 Côte de boeuf
17 Paleron
18 Macreuse

British

1 Knuckle
2 Shin
3 Brisket
4 Shoulder
5 Rolled ribs
6 Skirt
7 Aitchbone
8 Topside and silverside
9 Shin
10 Rump steak
11 Fillet
12 Baron or sirloin
13 Foreribs
14 Chuck/blade
15 Neck

American

1 Knuckle
2 Shank
3 Brisket
4 Rattleran
5 Short ribs
6 Flank
7 Aitchbone
8 Top round
9 Knuckle (soup bone)
10 Bottom round
11 Rump roast
12 Sirloin or rib steak
13 Tenderloin and Porterhouse (T bone)
14 Rib roast
15 Sirloin tip
16 Chuck or stewing steak

price. For example, those cast-iron cooking pots by Le Creuset are much cheaper in France but still pricey. The new non-stick versions are very popular and casseroles are superb. Omelette pans are good. But we find saucepans *very* heavy when full and have now built up a collection of copper saucepans (which is what our favourite restaurant chef uses). It is worth buying the best quality you can afford. The strongest are made in the perky little town in Normandy called, appropriately, Villedieu-les-Poêles (God's Town of the Frying Pans – the Knights of St John founded it and now it makes pans!). You can often buy secondhand saucepans in markets. Don't expect many lids. Our best buy recently were modern lids made of heatproof glass like Pyrex with ridges to fit different size saucepans. You can see through the top.

From ironmongers you can get wire whisks, much stronger than most, and strong 'chinois' – conical sieves (very useful). Glass and tableware are cheap in supermarkets. We buy plain white bowls for fruit and soup.

When you return home from France take chestnut purée (*purée de marrons*) plain and sweet – to make many dishes; and coffee beans to keep in the freezer (cheaper in France); various vegetables such as *flageolets* (dried or tinned), tins of *petits pois* (little peas), tiny string beans, artichokes, shallots (cheaper and fresher), and strings of garlic (keep them cool). Olive oil is sensationally cheaper, wine vinegar cheaper and better. Good quality tinned sauces are excellent but cheap ones are horrid. Some bakers and most hypermarkets sell frozen croissants. Take these home. Heated under the grill from frozen they taste like new!

Look for eau de vie (alcohol) marked 'pour conservations des fruits'. Take it as your spirit ration, pour it on to fresh fruit (peaches, plums, strawberries, raspberries, redcurrants) with a little sugar, in jars with tight lids, leave until Christmas for a fruit dessert and home-made liqueur.

2

EATING OUT

Fashions have altered attitudes and ingredients in French cooking. The great simple, balanced meals of great chefs like Carème and Escoffier gave way to so-called 'nouvelle cuisine' which made a very nice change for an occasional meal out when performed by a few great modern chefs. However, it became an expensive disaster when performed by lesser chefs who grossly overcharged for minute portions in decorative patterns. Nouvelle drifted into modern inventive or classical modern cooking which again produced a few seductive dishes from a few great chefs in extremely expensive restaurants which most of us can only afford when someone else pays the bill. But hundreds of aspiring young chefs have grabbed the chance to do their own thing or ape the Japanese, resulting in lukewarm dishes full of tasteless *mousselines* and puréed imitations of baby food with about as much taste. Who would have thought that the French would have ever put up with bland food, once associated with the Americans? No wonder Glyn Christian has asked if chefs have forgotten that their duty is to the palate, not the plate.

The race to be different has led to such bizarre mixtures as we have been offered lately – stewed rhubarb and scrambled egg and crayfish in courgette purée with slivers of kiwi fruit. The colour scheme is the only excuse. One starred young French chef excused the use of kiwi fruit so often because 'it has such a pretty colour'.

There is much food snobbery behind these fashions, as Egon Ronay points out, and the Young Aspiring Professionals, especially of Paris, are the most enthusiastic readers of the *Gault-Millau* guide. Few of us have the money or inclination to tour from one starred or toqued restaurant to another. In restaurants of *Logis de France* and *l'Auto-Journal* guide standards, old style and regional cooking is alive and well, with some dishes sensibly lightened for people who spend more time with their knees under a car wheel than walking. And blessedly regional traditions are returning even to the very serious restaurants. Arthur was proud when a brilliant young Michelin-starred chef asked him: 'If you know of any old regional recipes for this area, could you let me have them? That's going to be the next fashion.' We do hope that he is right.

For the young in France, of course, the fashion is hamburgers, Wimpys and fast foods eaten on the run. Pizza has been adopted as a French national dish.

Though appearing to be 'simple', modern dishes take time and although we know many, we have assumed that you will not want to spend time fiddling around the kitchen making decorative patterns with matchsticks of carrots and kiwi, three peas and a tomato aping a flower — time which you could spend seeking the hidden treasures of France. If you do want to spend a lot of time trying modern French dishes, take with you the Roux brothers' book *New Classical Cuisine* (Macdonald).

We have given some local recipes from each area of France, mostly easy and quick but with few which take longer for wet days or little dinner parties. These recipes were given to us over years locally not only by chefs but by housewives. Remember that basically the Loire divides France into, on the one hand, a northern land of much butter and little garlic and, on the other, the south with much garlic and mostly olive oil.

We have given also some simple basic recipes (like *Velouté Sauce*) in case you are like us and lose your memory when relaxing on holiday and need a few simple quick French dishes for busy days. We hope that, wherever you are staying, you will consider trying recipes from other areas. And do please take advantage of the gorgeous French vegetables. We serve them in summer cooked very lightly as complete meals, topped with a little butter, perhaps, or with cold meat from the charcuterie. If you want to do a lot of cooking, take the book used by all the younger members of our family *La Cuisine* (Orbis) written by the food writers of *Elle* magazine and translated into English by Jill Norman. It is very heavy, expensive and useful.

With superb olive oil, fresh vegetables including haricot and flageolet beans, fruit, nuts and noodles, France has no problems for vegetarians. There are health-food shops but, as elsewhere, most are packed with products of the lucrative health-food industry rather than fresh food. Margarine *ultra-légère* (light, whipped) is available and factory yoghurt, with dairy yoghurt in some areas – *fromage blanc* (fresh cream cheese) is slightly salted. *Fromage frais* is medium-fat cheese with the consistency of yoghurt. Cider vinegar of Normandy is excellent and wine vinegar is used much in cooking and marinades.

The French still love their white bread and although wholemeal bread (*pain intégral*, *entier* or *complet*) is becoming more popular, not all bakers sell it. *Pain de régime* is diet (low calorie) bread. Unleavened bread is *pain azyme*.

The *doux* (sweet) unsalted butter you now buy in shops is really lactic for it is pasteurised then reflavoured with lactic bacteria to replace the ones killed in pasteurisation. It is good for baking. Salt butter is only slightly salted. You can sometimes find unpasteurised butter (*beurre au lait cru* or *non-pasteurisé*) in markets. One farmer's wife usually sells it at the Saturday market in Dieppe and Philippe Olivier has it in his cheese shop in rue Thiers in Boulogne.

The justifiable reason for puréeing these lovely vegetables and fruits is for feeding a baby. You can buy the same tinned and bottled baby foods and packaged baby foods as you do at home, so worry about a baby should be about too much heat or sun, not feeding.

3

EATING IN

Our children are grown up now, but when they were young and we all went away for holidays where we were going to be in the same accommodation for a fortnight or more, we started by buying a big boiling fowl. We boiled it whole with carrots, onion, celery if available, one tomato, one big or two smaller leeks, bay leaf, a little thyme and parsley, pepper and a knuckle of greenback bacon.

This gave us one hot meal and lots of stock which we put in the fridge to skim off the fat and keep it. Next day we had slices of meat cold with local hams and a salad (dressed with walnut oil and with quartered walnuts in it). Any white meat left, we cut into thicker slices. Then we made a sauce with a knob of butter, four or five tablespoons of the stock and thick cream, flavoured perhaps at the last moment with a teaspoon or more of cranberry or redcurrant jelly. This sauce we poured over the chicken slices in a low foil dish, covered and put in the freezer or ice compartment of the fridge, where it would keep for a few days, to be reheated in the oven. The rest of the chicken we cut into cubes with diced bacon and carrot, moistened it with stock, added a bay leaf and made a chicken pie, using the chicken fat to make a short pastry, which was crispy and tasted of chicken and ham. Finally we broke up the carcass, added some more vegetables and seasoning, and boiled it with water and the rest of the stock for at least an hour, strained it, then either made it into soup or boiled it down further to make a strong stock for sauces. Either would last three days in the fridge, longer in a freezer compartment.

BASIC RECIPES

In your holiday mood you may forget how to make a dish — or even (as we sometimes do) forget one of the ingredients! You will find all you need in the Recipe section at the end of this book, where the dishes of each region are given. But here are some basic recipes which should cover most eventualities. (For four people in all cases.)

Béchamel Sauce

5 tablespoons butter
5 tablespoons flour
1 litre milk (preferably warmed)
medium-sized onion or shallots
small pinch of ground nutmeg
clove (optional)
small bouquet garni *(optional)*

White sauce used with fish, chicken, etc., and basis for many other sauces, such as Mornay (with cheese melted in), Soubise (with puréed onions).

Melt butter in heavy saucepan over medium-low heat. Add flour, stir hard with wooden spoon until butter absorbs flour completely. Cook, stirring, for 3 to 5 minutes. Remove from heat, pour in milk, stirring continually. Return saucepan to heat, bring slowly to the boil, stirring. Cook over gentle heat for 10 minutes. Add nutmeg, salt and pepper to taste.

If you like, now peel and dice onion, add it with a clove and *bouquet garni* to sauce, simmer for 30 minutes, stirring frequently. Strain.

Bouquet Garni

Herbs for soup, stews, fish stock, etc., in a bunch or preferably muslin bag — often thyme, parsley, bay leaf, peppercorns.

Court-Bouillon

1 litre dry white wine
1 litre water
3 tablespoons white wine vinegar (optional)
1 celery stalk or white of leek or both
2 large onions
sprig of thyme
bunch of parsley
6 peppercorns (black if possible)
2 cloves (optional)
1 clove garlic (optional)
1 large carrot

For poaching fish, such as salmon, trout.

Peel and slice carrot and onions; cut celery into pieces. Put everything into a large saucepan with salt to taste. Bring to boil, simmer 40 to 60 minutes. Let it cool before straining. Keeps for months in freezer, days in fridge.

Fumet de poisson (fish stock)

750g fish trimmings (heads, etc)
2 large onions
white of leek
2 carrots
bouquet garni
½ lemon
250ml white wine
1 litre water

The basis of most fish sauces.

Peel and finely chop vegetables, cut lemon in half, roughly crush fish trimmings. Put all in big saucepan with salt and pepper. Bring to boil. Simmer 60 minutes. Strain (will keep 2 to 3 days in fridge – months in freezer).

Pâte feuilletée quatre tours (puff pastry)

500g plain flour, plus flour for dusting
400 to 500g firm butter (more butter means richer pastry)
200ml water
2 teaspoons salt (some French chefs add 2 tablespoons white wine vinegar)

Put flour on working surface, make a well in the middle. Pour in water, vinegar, salt and 50g of the melted butter. Mix into a smooth paste, roll into a ball, put into refrigerator for at least 30 minutes. Put the rest of the butter in the fridge, too. Flour the work surface. Roll out the ball of dough into a round 2cm thick. Cut remaining butter into small pieces and spread it in the centre of the dough round. Flatten butter with rolling pin until it is spread thickly over the pastry. Fold pastry in three to envelope the butter completely. Seal with a rolling pin. Roll out again to distribute butter evenly. Fold into three and roll away from you into a rectangle. Dust surface with flour. Turn pastry 90 degrees. Fold into three and roll into rectangle again. Put in fridge for 15-30 minutes to harden up. Remove it and fold and roll twice more. You have now completed four turns (*quatre tours*) but two more turns are recommended! If not used immediately, it will keep wrapped in polythene for 3 to 4 days in fridge, 2 months in freezer. Each time you take it out of the fridge, leave it 10 to 15 minutes at room temperature before rolling to let butter melt a bit. This prevents it breaking up.

Sauce Velouté

2 tablespoons butter
1 tablespoon flour
150ml chicken or veal stock
cooking liquid from dish to be accompanied or if necessary milk
2 egg yolks
125ml thick cream
lemon juice

Basic cream white sauce, used as it is, flavoured or as a basis for cream soups.

Melt butter in saucepan, add flour and cook for 2 minutes, stirring. Put in liquid, stirring well. Bring to boil, then simmer for 2 minutes over gentle heat. Leave to cool a little, mix egg yolks with cream and add. Season with salt and pepper, add a few drops of lemon juice. Cook stirring, without boiling, until thick and smooth.

QUICK OR SIMPLE DISHES

Cabillaud au Muscadet (cod in white wine)

4 cod steaks (about 150g each)
4 medium tomatoes
4 shallots
40g butter
½ litre dry white wine
2 tablespoons chopped fresh parsley (persil) *and tarragon (*estragon*) or all parsley*
2 tablespoons thick cream
lemon juice
½ bay leaf
*pinch of dried thyme (*thym*)*

Heat oven (to 200°C, 400°F, Mark 6). Peel and slice shallots. Peel tomatoes, take out seeds, chop flesh. Soften shallots in butter over medium heat. Pour them and butter into ovenproof dish. Add tomatoes, thyme, bay leaf. Put cod in dish in one layer, salt and pepper, then pour over the wine. Put in oven until wine starts to boil, turn heat off and leave dish inside for 5 minutes more. Remove cod steaks and keep hot in ovenproof dish. Pour the rest into a saucepan and boil hard until half liquid evaporates. Put it through a strainer into another saucepan, pressing vegetables to extract juices. Add cream, a few drops of lemon juice and reheat. Coat the fish with this sauce and heat in the oven until the sauce starts to simmer. Sprinkle with chopped parsley and tarragon.

Céleri Salade à la Roquefort (celery salad with blue cheese sauce)

2 heads of celery
125 to 150g chopped walnuts
125g Roquefort or other softish blue cheese
1 tablespoon Cognac
4 tablespoons walnut oil
1 tablespoon wine vinegar
salt
pepper

Trim celery, remove tough strings, slice finely into a bowl. Add walnuts. Crush cheese with fork, mash it in Cognac, add oil, vinegar and salt and pepper (remember that cheese is salty). Pour dressing over the celery.

Concombres au Gratin (cucumber in cheese sauce)

*3 cucumbers (*concombres*)*
1 onion finely chopped
2 tablespoons butter
2 tablespoons flour
200ml crème fraîche *(slightly sour cream from shops — or use thick cream)*
50g grated cheese (Gruyère, Emmental or similar)
small pinch nutmeg

Serve as a starter, snack or vegetable with meat or chicken.

Preheat oven (to 220°C, 425°F, Mark 7). Peel cucumbers, cut lengthwise into quarters; remove seeds, cube flesh. Add cucumber cubes to a pan of boiling salted water, blanch for 10 minutes. Drain and place in shallow oven dish. Heat butter in a saucepan, cook onion gently until soft but not brown. Sprinkle in the flour, mix well, then add cream, stirring constantly until mixture has thickened. Stir in grated cheese, nutmeg, pepper and salt to taste. Pour sauce over the cucumber. Bake for 20 minutes until top is brown.

Croque Signor (veal escalopes stuffed with cheese)

4 veal escalopes (about 150g each)
4 thin slices gruyère (or similar) cheese
2 eggs
4 tablespoons dry breadcrumbs

Cut veal pieces through so that they can be opened like a book — not right through. Brush inside with oil, slip in the cheese and close. Cut off any cheese which sticks out. Beat eggs, coat veal with eggs, then breadcrumbs. Sprinkle with salt and pepper. Heat rest of oil in frying pan, add veal escalopes. Cook over medium heat, covered for 5 to 6 minutes on each side (until golden brown).

Emincé de Boeuf

750g rump or boneless sirloin steak
2 onions finely chopped
40g butter
250ml crème fraîche *or double cream*
1 teaspoon Dijon mustard

'Emincé' means cut in strips — not minced. These are in mustard sauce.

Trim fat from steak, cut into slices 5mm thick. Cut these slices into 5mm strips. Heat half the butter, add half the meat strips, cook over high heat, stirring, until brown all over. Remove and cook other half. Heat the rest of the butter in the pan, add onions and cook until soft and translucent. Add cream until mixture is clear and golden, then add mustard, season with salt and lots of pepper. Bring to boil and cook stirring until sauce thickens. Add meat strips and any juice from them, heat quickly but do not allow to boil. Serve immediately.

Entrecôtes Bercy (sirloin steaks in Bercy sauce)

4 boneless rib steaks (sirloin or entrecôte *— about 200 to 250g each)*
4 shallots
1/4 bottle dry white wine
2 tablespoons oil
4 tablespoons butter
bunch of fresh parsley chopped

Chop shallots finely. Cook them in the wine with salt and pepper on medium heat until 3 tablespoons of liquid remain. Brush steaks with oil and grill 3 to 4 minutes on each side. Season. Add chopped parsley to reduced sauce and butter, cut into small pieces, whisking hard. Serve steaks coated with sauce.

Gratin de Poires (pear gratin)

1 kg pears
100g sugar
80g butter
3 tablespoons double cream

Most French desserts include wine, spirits or are loaded with butter or syrup. This uses a reasonable amount.

Peel pears, cut in quarters and take out core. Arrange in ovenproof dish, sprinkle with sugar, dot with butter. Add a little water. Put in oven (heated to 220°C, 425°F, Mark 7). When juice is caramel colour, take out, add cream and serve.

Omelette au Plat à Tomate (baked tomato omelette)

10-12 eggs
50g grated cheese (gruyère or similar)
1 tablespoon chopped parsley or chives
3 middle-sized tomatoes
50g butter

Heat oven (to 220°C, 425°F, Mark 7). Beat eggs with salt, pepper, cheese and parsley. Skin tomatoes by plunging in boiling water for 10 seconds then in cold (the skins will almost fall off), then slice. Heat butter in ovenproof dish. Arrange tomato slices over the bottom of the dish, cover with egg mixture. Bake for 15 minutes. Thin slices of any hard salami-type sausage or small squares of ham or bacon can be mixed with the tomatoes.

Smoked Salmon Soufflé Roll

For souffle: 250ml milk
2 tablespoons flour
2 tablespoons butter
4 egg yolks
*2 tablespoons fresh chopped chives (*ciboulettes*)*
6 egg whites
*For filling: 180ml sour cream (*crème aigre*) or thick cream plus 3 drops of vinegar*
100g smoked salmon, diced small

Recipe of Madame Monmousseau of the sparkling wine family from Montrichard in the Loire

Preheat oven (to 180°C, 350°F, Mark 4). Line soufflé dish or shallow pan (about 25cm × 38cm × 2.5cm) with foil, buttered. Melt butter in small saucepan over medium heat; add flour, stirring constantly, to make a smooth roux. Add milk gradually, stirring fast, until mixture thickens and boils.

Remove from heat and cool for 5 minutes. Add yolks, beating well. Beat egg whites with pinch of salt until stiff. Fold into soufflé base. Bake in oven for 20 minutes or until puffy and set. Wait 5 minutes and turn out onto a damp kitchen cloth. Spread the cream over the inside, leaving a 2 to 3cm border. Sprinkle smoked salmon evenly over the top. Roll up carefully, like a Swiss roll, transfer carefully to serving dish, sprinkle with chives and serve in slices, or wrap in foil and keep warm for an hour. Served cold, it is a little heavier but just as tasty.

Steak aux Trois Fromages (hamburgers with three cheeses)

750g minced steak
6 tablespoons cream cheese
3 to 4 tablespoons grated parmesan
6 tablespoons grated gruyère or similar
3 tablespoons chopped fresh parsley
pinch of grated nutmeg
4 tablespoons oil

Mix well cream cheese and steak. Add other cheeses, parsley, nutmeg, salt and pepper. Mix together with your hands. Divide into four equal portions and shape into 'hamburgers'. Heat oil in frying pan, cook hamburgers 3-4 minutes on each side.

Vichyssoise (chilled leek and potato soup)

1 litre chicken stock
4 leeks (white part)
4 onions
5 medium potatoes
3 tablespoons butter
150ml double cream or crème fraîche
150ml white wine (optional)
3 tablespoons chopped chives (optional)

Milk or some milk can be used if chicken stock not available, but is not quite so good.

Chop leeks and onions finely, cook them in melted butter over gentle heat for 15 minutes. Do not let them brown. Peel and thinly slice potatoes. Add to pan and cook 3 minutes, stirring. Bring stock or milk to the boil. Add vegetables and wine. Cook for 20 minutes or until potatoes are really soft. Purée in machine or with a whisk, and strain. Leave to cool. Add cream and whisk vigorously. Add salt and pepper to taste. Chill in fridge until ready to serve. Sprinkle with chopped chives.

4

WINES

Bad weather, inflation, the still-too-high dollar and the climbing yen have rocketed prices of classic wines which we all know or know about. Médoc wines like Margaux, Pauillac, other Bordeaux such as Pomerol and St Emilion, the wines of the great Burgundy wine road from Gevrey-Chambertin through Beaune to Meursault and the villages of Beaujolais, great Rhône wines like Châteauneuf du Pape and Hermitage, the whites of Chablis, Sancerre and Pouilly-sur-Loire, not to mention Pouilly Fuissé, have become wines for special meals and celebrations. Now is the time to copy the French themselves and make new friends among wines.

There are new wine fashions in France. Paris is discovering wines which many foreigners have enjoyed for a long time. Bourgueil, the red from the Loire, like a rustic Médoc, Gigondas, the Rhône red which can be every bit as good as Châteauneuf du Pape, Cahors, the deep-coloured, strong wine of Quercy popular with our grandfathers but 'discovered' only lately by the French, Bergerac red of the Dordogne, not far away from the Bordeaux wine country, have all had recent fashions. Now Chinon, the soft Loire red, is being bought by French hotel-keepers instead of the pricey St Emilion, and Bandol, quite the best red of Provence, has been discovered.

The French call lesser-known wines *Vins de Pays*. They are mostly drunk locally by tourists or local people. These wines are produced in a defined area from specified grape varieties. If you are anywhere near a wine area, these are worth seeking.

We would avoid blended table wines 'vins de table' — unless you are throwing a party for people who want to get drunk. These wines tend to be sold in supermarkets at the lowest prices. Whilst supermarkets often do have some good special offers, and are useful in areas where wine is not produced, it seems perverse, if not stupid, to seek supermarket blended 'plonk' or inferior wines from elsewhere when one can buy local wine for everyday drinking. General storage and handling too leaves much to be desired – we have seen cases of wine left standing in the sun around the back of supermarkets. We would not buy medium grade or good wines from a supermarket if we could find a reasonably priced wine shop.

Try the local named wines, preferably those marked *Appellation d'origine Contrôlée*. This AOC (or AC as it is more commonly known) is an official classification which is not infallible but fairly reliable. Because of big improvements in culture and winemaking in many parts of France, there are more wines deserving the AC classification which do not have it than wines given an appellation which do not deserve it. It is well worth studying their labels – if only for the date – because it helps to decide whether the wine you are buying is really too old – a common fault, for many *Vins de Pays* lose flavour and especially their grapey taste if kept for more than a year or two. Others, of course, can be a bit like battery acid if not kept long enough. Very few wines below the AC level are worth keeping more than 2 to 3 years, and not all AC wines.

Just below the AC level you will find some very drinkable wines marked 'VDQS' (*Vin Délimité de Qualité Supérieure*). These wines are grown and made under strict rules and also have to undergo an annual 'blind' tasting by experts.

At the top of AC classification, wines are given different categories in each area. When to drink them is a matter of constant discussion but the French, for example, tend to drink good Bordeaux red wines younger than visitors do, and most ordinary Frenchmen therefore prefer Burgundy, which basically matures quicker. Dry white wine is usually drunk young (1 to 3 years) when it is fresh, grapey and slightly acidic. Exceptions include grand and premier cru Chablis, most of the other great white Burgundies such as Pouilly Fuissé and Meursault and many Vouvray, including 1985 wines.

Some classifications even decide the best temperature to serve the wine. According to the producers in Beaujolais, wines classified simply as Beaujolais or Beaujolais Villages should be drunk young and fairly cold (around 14°C or 58°F) while the Grand Cru wines of the nine named villages such as Fleurie, Brouilly and Juliénas can mostly be kept longer to improve (especially Moulin-à-Vent) and are served at room temperature (*chambré*).

The nicest way to buy wine in wine-producing areas is from local co-operatives in bottles or *vrac* (a large plastic container with taps) or from the producers themselves. Look for notices saying 'Dégustation', 'Dégustation des Vins' or 'Dégustation et Vente Directe' and follow the arrow. You can taste the wines. Obviously they hope to sell you wine, so we always buy one bottle at least. This is the best way to taste wine, anyway – with the right meal! We also buy a *vrac* or two to take home and bottle there if we have room in the car. It is worth paying customs duty if you get the right wine – not worth paying duty on plonk. We have bought and bottled at home a wine which cost, including duty and VAT, half what it would have cost us in most home wine merchants. Arthur's new book which gives names and locations of hundreds of places where you can taste wines around France, mostly country wines, will be published just after this book – *Eperon's French Wine Tour* (Pan).

5

NORMANDY

The cows cud-chewing in the lush meadows of Normandy are no longer all traditional brown and white and most cream, butter and cheese are produced in factories, not farm dairies. But cream, cider and the apple spirit called Calvados are still used lavishly in Norman kitchens, surviving the raspberry vinegar and kiwi fruit revolution and the fibre fashion. We can remember when old Norman farmers put bowls of thick cream on their tables and ladled it into soup. Cooking remains classical and regional, sometimes rustic – and none the worse for that.

Local markets are a joy in Normandy. Here you can buy the real farm produce and fish freshly landed. Dieppe's Saturday morning market, spilling out from Grand'Rue into side roads, is a revelation in these days of EEC conformity. We have bought the best butter in France there, from slabs straight from farm dairies, the cheapest oysters, some of the best-made cheeses. Dieppe has a daily fish market, too. Other good fish markets are at Fécamp and charming Honfleur, and two inland at Rouen (an important port on the Seine) and Caen.

The most popular local fish are sole, turbot and *barbue* (brill, a lesser turbot, which the French like and we don't). Mussels, *praires* (clams) and oysters are favourite shellfish,

Clams

Oysters

though *coquilles Saint-Jacques* (scallops) are used a lot, so are *crevettes* (*gris* are shrimps, *roses* are prawns). Cherbourg has superb langoustines called *Demoiselles*. Succulent oysters come from the charming village of Vaast La Hougue east of Cherbourg. In true old *sole à la Normande*, the sole is poached in cider and cream. Most chefs outside Normandy cook the sole in wine, then add the cream to make a sauce.

Sole à la Dieppoise is delicious. Originally cider was used, but even Normans often use wine these days (see recipe). *Sauce Normande* takes many forms, too, but for fish you use a fish-stock based *velouté sauce*, fish *fumet* and cream, and it is hardly worth so much holiday time. For *matelote Dieppoise*, fish and shellfish are stewed in cider with leeks, then cream and Calvados added.

There is little local beef in Normandy but plenty of field veal, especially from the lush and pretty Vallée d'Auge, where cows graze beside apple orchards and the best cider and Calvados are made. Excellent chickens are bred here. *Poulet Vallée d'Auge* produced outside Normandy can be any old chicken cooked in cider with cream added. Here everyone has their favourite recipe, but all are rich in cream (see recipe).

Rouen ducks are a special breed (crossed domestic and wild, with a touch of Barbary) and come mostly from Yvetot and Duclair. To make the restaurant dish *caneton à la Rouennaise*, the duck has to be killed to keep its blood and you need a special press to squeeze it from the carcass. The duck is stuffed with its liver, lightly roasted, then squeezed. Juices, blood and cream are used in the sauce.

The salt marshes around the Cherbourg peninsula produce *pré-salé* lamb. Shoulder cooked in cider, cream and Calvados is delicious (*Epaule à la Crème*).

Game is plentiful in the land of wild hills, woods and fast streams west of Vire (called La Suisse Normande) especially pheasant, partridge, woodcock and trout. Game birds are usually flambéed in Calvados (see recipe). Pork is produced all over Normandy but especially where skimmed milk is available to feed the pigs. Charcuteries sell a big *andouillette* chitterling sausage from Vire to serve cold and sliced as a starter. For cooking meat, Normans used traditionally *graisse Normande*, made by clarifying equal amounts of pork fat and suet, flavoured with vegetables and herbs. You can buy it in cardboard pots in some butchers and charcuteries. Most Normans now buy tripe *à la mode de Caen* in glass pots from a Charcuterie. It's a simple dish, but it takes 8 to 10 hours to cook.

The great local sweet, *Bourdelots Normands*, is whole apple baked in suet crust (apple dumplings). When pears are used they are called *douillons*.

Each cook has his own way of making Norman apple tart. Arthur was taught to make it in a Dieppe cookery school by half filling a pastry flan with cooking apples stewed in cider and sugar, then whisked to a mousse. This was topped with overlapping slices of eating apples sprinkled with Calvados and sugar. Then the flan was baked. When cool it was glazed with apricot jam. Old-timers used Calvados for glaze. You can usually buy apple tart in pâtisseries. It has to be served covered in cream, of course! Another delicious dessert from a pâtisserie is *mirliton*, a puff pastry tart, filled with yolks of egg, sugar and vanilla blended over heat until brown, then baked for 15 minutes. For 250g of pastry use 125g butter, 50g of sugar, inside of a vanilla pod (or ½ teaspoon of vanilla extract). Chefs also add ½ tablespoon of orange blossom water or ½ teaspoon of orange extract.

CHEESES

Normandy is truly rich in cheeses. Camembert came originally from a hamlet of that name in the Pays d'Auge. It was invented in 1790 by a farm wife, Marie Harel, whose statue stands in nearby Vimoutiers, donated by an American cheese company. Farm Camembert is scarce but you may get it in a market. Otherwise, it pays to buy the best, costing only a few francs more a box. Strong, pungent, spicey Livarot is delicious, and scarce because it is made mainly on farms (best May-February). Brillat-Savarin is mild and very creamy – factory made. Pont L'Evêque, soft and sweet, gets its criss-crossed crust by drying on straw matting.

Other cheeses (all cow's) are: Trappiste de Bricquebec or Providence (soft, yellow, robust; made in the monastery); Bondon de Neufchatel which takes many shapes, eaten either fresh (*fleuri*) or strong and ripe (*affiné*); Carré de Bray (soft, salty, mushroom smell); Coeur de Bray (soft, supple, fruity); Demi-sel (small, moist, creamy, wrapped in paper); Petits-Suisses (rich, fresh, fluffy cream cheese, unsalted, paper wrapped); Pavé d'Auge (spicy, tangy square with yellow rind).

DRINKS

No wine is made in Normandy. Calvados (apple spirit) is strong with distinctive apple flavour. Traditionally drunk in the middle of a meal (*Trou Normand* – Norman hole) to settle the digestion. It works! Posher restaurants now serve it over apple or *Calvados sorbet* (water ice). Benedictine, fragrant liqueur of Fécamp, was first made by a monk in 1510 from cliffside herbs. Now made in a Fécamp factory which you can visit (from Easter to mid-November, every day, 9.00 to 11.15 a.m. and 2.00 to 6 p.m. In winter Monday to Friday only).

Cider is very dry (*brut/sec*) or sweet (*doux*). It is often still fermenting in the bottle (*cidre bouché*). Most is factory made, but at Longueville it is made traditionally, under the brand name Le Duc. You can also buy *poiré* (perry) made from pears.

6

PICARDY & THE NORTH

Gastronomes sometimes sneer patronisingly at the simple 'peasant' food of Picardy and the North. The Flemish influence in the cooking upsets Parisians. But there is little wrong with good plain cooking of good fresh ingredients.

Beef from Picardy is underrated. Pork is good and plentiful. Salt-meadow (*pré-salé*) lamb from the Somme estuary is nearly up to Normandy flavour, and sea fish — shellfish, herring, mackerel, cod, turbot and monkfish (*lotte*) — are superb, especially when freshly-landed on the fish quay at Boulogne, France's biggest fishing port.

Heavier vegetables grown in the market gardens round the waterways near St Omer are some of the finest in France. So, once again, do not buy your vegetables in the supermarket but in the local shop or especially the weekly market.

Leeks, cauliflower, sprouts (picked young), carrots (dug young), excellent potatoes and chicory (which the French call 'endive' and can be delicious) are all grown here. Asparagus is plentiful in season. The Flemish way is to serve it hot with

Asparagus

melted butter and hot, hard-boiled eggs cut in half. You mash your own egg into the butter (*asperges à la Flamande*).

The oddest vegetable is *jets de houblon* (hop shoots). The female hops are used to make beer. The male flowers are edible and are broken away from the woody stem. They are boiled in salt water with a little lemon juice, then tossed in butter or tossed in butter then simmered in fresh cream. Alas, modern methods of growing hops are making the male rare in the hop gardens. They can be served garnished with poached eggs and fried-bread croutons.

Get away from motorways and main roads and you can find some delightful villages hidden secretively among wooded hills and rich pastures, with inland waterways rich in pike, eels large and small (*anguilles* and *anguillettes*) and trout. Tinned *quennelles*, made locally, can be bought in épiceries and charcuteries (*quennelles de brochet*) and can be light as soufflé. You can also buy *cervelais de brochet* (slender sausage of pike and potatoes).

Trout from the River Canche are still delicious, but some are farmed alongside the river. On the charming little N 127 road through the Canche valley between Desvres and Montreuil-sur-Mer is a riverside farm where you can buy the freshest trout – or catch your own.

If you are anywhere near Boulogne, you should be able to buy fine fresh fish. Mussels are very often some of the best in

Mussels

the world. They are usually cooked the most popular way in France – *à la Marinière* – in wine with chopped onion, parsley and bay leaf. There are fewer herrings and mackerel to smoke these days, but Boulogne still produces various types of salted and smoked, probably the best in France. They include *craquelots* (or *bouffs*) – small herrings cured for a few hours over walnut or hazelnut leaves, also produced in Dunkirk; lightly smoked, called 'demi-sel' or 'doux'; also kippers, smoked more lightly than elsewhere and *harengs saurs* (salted and smoked, sometimes called 'gendarmes'). In

Calais, you can sometimes buy herrings or mackerel already stuffed with soft roes and herbs and baked in paper cases (*hareng à la Calaisienne*). At Boulogne, fresh fish is sold daily on the fish quay. Smoked herrings or mackerel pâté is excellent here. Little harbour fish are nice fried (*friture du port*).

Boulogne's market is held every Wednesday and Saturday 7.00 a.m. to 1.00 p.m. in Place Dalton, around the old St Nicholas church. It is good for vegetables, pâté, charcuterie but especially cheeses. You may know this square for two bistros – Chez Jules and Alfred. Running into it is rue Thiers, with Philippe Olivier's superb cheese shop with maturing cellars containing 200 cheeses, mostly from farms, not factories. The Calais food markets are in Place d'Armes (square with a tower) on Wednesday and Saturday mornings and Place Crèvecoeur (off Boulevard Lafayette, up the hill past the railway station and town hall) on Thursday and Saturday mornings. Dunkirk's market is in Place du Théâtre on Wednesday and Saturday mornings.

Charcuteries sell very good pork products, especially smoked sausages. Arras is known for *andouillettes*, Valenciennes for smoked tongue, Péronne for eel pâté. You might find *crabe chausson* (crab meat baked in pastry). Duck pâtés and *ballotines* are excellent. You might be lucky enough to find in a posher charcuterie a genuine *pâté de caneton d'Amiens* – the great gastronomic dish of Picardy. It is a duck ballotine (originally with the bones in it, now usually boned). The duck is fried whole, surrounded by a forcemeat of duck and chicken liver, fat bacon, onion and herbs, wrapped in pastry, baked and served cold in slices. Delicious!

Amiens produces almond macaroons. Lille makes biscuits (*petits beurres, gauffes fourrés*). Dunkirk produces many cakes and biscuits, including *kokeboterom* (sweet bun dotted with raisins).

CHEESES

The cheeses include Maroilles, a tangy, smelly, super cheese, in small slabs with orange brown rind, creamy inside; made originally by monks in Maroilles monastery 1,000 years ago. Mashed with herbs and pepper and shaped into a cone, it becomes *boulette d'Avesnes*. Mashed with herbs and matured in crocks, it becomes *fort Béthunes*. Gris de Lille, made mostly by small dairies and farms, is an acquired taste. In a slab with a sticky pink-grey rind, it is cured in brine and beer and is very strong in smell and taste. Known also as *gris puant* (grey stinky), *puant de Lille*, or *puant macéré* (stinky pickled). Dauphin, named after Louis XIV's son, is soft, smooth, herb-flavoured and smelly but very nice.

DRINKS

The only wine produced is a tiny amount in Aisne, just over the Champagne border. It is beef country and, in Flemish style, much beer is used in cooking. Juniper berries and Dutch gin are also used. Flemish dishes include *flamiche* (or *flamique*) – leek tart in different versions (see recipe); carbonnade Flamande – beef braised in beer (see recipe); chou rouge à la Flamande – red cabbage with apples (see recipe); beer soup (see recipe); *hochepot* – another dish with many versions but usually a 'soup-stew' with brisket of beef, bacon, pigs' ears, breast and shoulder of mutton or lamb, cooked with mixed sliced vegetables such as cabbage, carrots, onions, leeks and potatoes, served like *pot au feu* – the liquid as soup, meat and vegetables as another course; carrot flan Flamande can be served hot or cold (see recipe). *Ficelles Picardes* are pancakes stuffed with chopped ham and mushrooms in cream (similar to *Ficelles Normandes*; sometimes cheese is used instead of cream).

7

BRITTANY

As the sea dominates Brittany, the sea harvest dominates Breton tables. Superb fish is sold in fascinating markets in towns and villages all round the coast. Nearly every sort of shellfish is landed – lobster, *langoustines*, crabs, large clams (*palourdes*), small clams (*praires*), winkles (*bigorneaux*), outstanding mussels. Oysters are farmed at Cancale and Morlaix in the north and in the river estuaries of the Bélon and Peneurf, mussels between the Rance estuary and Cape Fréhel. Apart from St Malo, the big fishing ports are on the south coast – Concarneau, Lorient, Douarnenez, Camaret, Quiberon, St Guénolé. St Malo is the port for cod. Tunny and sardines are landed in season, and there is usually plenty of sole, plaice, turbot and brill. Quimper has an excellent market for all food from sea and country.

The Breton national dish, apart from pancakes, is *cotriade* – a stew of white fish, mussels, often eels, with onions, potatoes, herbs and cream, and any other vegetables (celery, tomatoes) and often white wine.

Clams are stuffed with chopped shallots, garlic and herbs mixed with butter, then baked or grilled. They can be delicious. You can often buy them stuffed, ready to bake, at a fish shop or in charcuteries (*palourdes* or *praires farcies*).

The Armoricaine sauce served mostly with lobster (*homard à l'Armoricaine*) but sometimes with other fish is not a traditional Breton sauce and you are more likely to be served it in a superior or tourist restaurant than in a local restaurant or Breton home. It is made of cream, wine, onions, garlic, tomatoes and herbs. The lobster is usually sautéed in oil, then flambéed in brandy. There are arguments about the origin of the sauce but the most likely story we heard in Brittany was that it was invented by the chef at the Breton

Lobster

pavilion at the Great Paris Exposition of 1867 who named it after Armorica, the old name for Britanny. Then a Paris chef muddled everything by calling the dish 'homard à l'Americaine'. Well made, the sauce is excellent. You can buy it in tins in supermarkets or some charcuteries, but we have found this version fairly horrible.

In Brittany, haddock, called *aiglefin* elsewhere, is called 'anon'. An interesting freshwater fish in Brittany is burbot, with long dorsal and tail fins, sometimes called *lotte de rivière* (river monkfish). It is a Breton delicacy (see recipe). Rivers also offer carp, shad, eel and pike (*brochet*) – served often with *beurre blanc* (see recipe). Salmon from Odet and Aunis rivers are rare but excellent.

Fish is so dominant that you could miss the fine land-produced food. Beef-dairy cattle produce butter almost of Normandy standard. Lamb from the sea-washed meadows (*pré-salé*) is delicious and expensive. Favourite ways of serving lamb are *gigot* (or *épaule*) *de pré-salé à la Bretonne* (leg of lamb, or shoulder, with white beans) and *côtes d'agneau à l'estragon* (lamb chops with tarragon).

Brittany is the biggest producer of pigs in France and charcuteries are full of sausages and pork products. *Andouille Bretonne* (soft pork chitterling sausage) is often fatty. Pork and smoked sausage are used in Breton hot pot (*potée Bretonne*) (see recipe). So is chicken. Brittany produces a third of France's home-produced chickens. Nantes area produces excellent duck and also turkeys. Duck is served with cherry sauce (*caneton Nantais aux cerises*).

For generations Brittany has been known for onions (from around Roscoff) and lovely early kidney-shaped potatoes (we are surprised that the EEC bureaucrats have not banned these, as they have done to the superb Epicure potatoes). The area behind Concarneau and Lorient produces excellent peas and French beans, the rich alluvial soil near St Malo and of the Loire north of Nantes encourages market gardens specialising in young carrots and cauliflowers, and cauliflowers come from the Roscoff-Morlaix area, which also produces superb large-type globe artichokes. They are usually boiled and eaten leaf by leaf, dipped in melted butter, or vinaigrette when cold. Try boiling potatoes with onions, butter, salt and a piece of salt pork (*pommes petit salé*). Or opening up a cucumber, taking out the seeds and stuffing with chopped cooked carrots, peas and egg (*concombres farcis*). *Bardatte* is stuffed cabbage (see recipe). Delicious strawberries come from Plougastel.

Crêpes (pancakes) are a Breton way of life. *Crêperies* are everywhere, some just beachside stalls, some big restaurants. Usually *crêpes* are made with sugar and served with fruit, jam or cream fillings. Bretons like to eat them with cider or *lait baratté* (buttermilk) around the late afternoon. Made with salt they are filled with cheese, bacon, fried egg or a mixture of these and become a snack lunch or supper. The original savoury version is made with buckwheat flour and called a *galette*. You can buy *crêpes* in packets or by the dozen in boulangeries or pâtisseries and they can be reheated in butter or oil, but they are easy to make fresh, even if not as superbly as in some *crêperies* (see recipe).

Crêpes dentelles are thin-as-lace crispy biscuits made in Quimperlé. Served with ice-cold whipped cream, they make a superb light dessert. In pâtisseries you can buy *pommes beignets* (apple doughnuts), *konign-amman* (light coffee-streaked cake), *bigouden* (rice and almond biscuits).

CHEESES

Two very similar fresh cream cheeses are usually eaten as dessert with fruit, jam or sprinkled with sugar. They are *crémet Nantais* and *maingaux Rennais*. Other cheeses – fromage du curé or Nantais (small, soft, mild); Trappiste de Campénéac (yellow, supple cheese in large discs with yellowish rind – made by nuns at a convent); St Agathon (local Guingamp cow's milk cheese; small, round and available October-July); Abbaye de la Meilleraye (large square slab with ochre rind; tangy, supple and available May-February).

WINES

Brittany is cider country, although not of Normandy standards. The best is from Fouesnant. Cidre bouché is fizzy because still fermenting. But Nantes, now technically part of the Loire, is regarded by Bretons as part of Brittany (it was capital of the old Duchy of Brittany when it was separate from France). So Bretons regard the wine made around Nantes as their own – Muscadet (made from the grape of that name; dry, fruity wine served mostly with fish, more recently fashionable in Paris as an aperitif). Gros Plant (coarser dry white, crisper and more acidic; made from *folle-blanche* grapes). Coteaux d'Ancenis is VDQS (superior wine from a definite district – it is white, light, refreshing or red, like a light and very ordinary Beaujolais).

8

PARIS & ÎLE DE FRANCE

Food from the world comes into Paris (even frozen chickens from Maryland). Les Halles, moved to Rungis near Orly airfield, is the biggest food market in the world, with one whole pavilion devoted to sausages. So it seems naïve to talk about 'fresh local ingredients'.

But Paris is still girdled by the countryside of Île de France. Despite 'son of Corbusier' suburbs looking like forts, the tarmac of Orly covering fields which once produced superb little potatoes and De Gaulle airfield covering square kilometres which grew superb artichokes, cherries and *morels* (the tastiest of mushrooms), Île de France still has the best market gardens outside Brittany and the Loire. Their produce may be rarer and therefore dearer, but you can still get it and it is always worth asking for the produce by the name of the area famous for it. Ask for asparagus of Argenteuil, green peas of Clamart, French beans of Bagnolet, superb green *flageolet* kidney beans of Arpajon, south of Paris, which once had their own railway to take them to Les Halles.

Artichoke

Artichokes and asparagus come from around Laon. Noyon, just past Compiègne, produces white beans named after nearby Soissons. Lettuces are grown round Versailles. The superb little carrots of Crécy-sur-Morin are used in many dishes, including the soup *potage Crécy* (we thought for years, like many other foreigners, that they came from Crécy in the Somme where the Black Prince and his archers whipped the French in 1346).

For two centuries little white mushrooms were grown around Paris and in caves under the pavements of the very suburbs. With much rebuilding in the 1960s and the spread of suburbs most growers moved to caves in the Loire and we know of no growers in Paris now. But most dishes called '*à la Parisienne*' nearly always include these white mushrooms which are still called *champignons de Paris*.

The old royal hunting forests of Compiègne and Fontainebleau are still beautiful and still rich in game; venison, wild boar, hare, rabbit, partridge and pheasant are made into delicious pâtés and charcuterie. We have given a recipe for *terrine de gibier* (game *terrine*) which should last a few days for starters or snacks. You can use any game but it is best with strong game, such as boar, although we have used it successfully for years with pheasant.

Charcuteries are varied and excellent, with pork predominating. You can buy *jambon glacé de Paris* (slightly smoked, boned and cooked ham), *boudins noirs et blancs* (black and white pudding), *petit salé* (lightly salted roast pork), *pâté de foie de cochon* (pig's liver pâté), *fromage de tête de porc* (brawn), *hure de porc à la Parisienne* (pork tongue in jelly), *friands Parisiens* (little light sausage rolls).

Paris butchers are brilliant at cutting meat, even by French standards. A rare, expensive but succulent and delicious meat is field veal from Pontoise. Much of the *longe de veau Pontoise* served in restaurants is any veal cooked in the Pontoise manner – loin of veal braised in white wine with carrots and onions. That is nice, too.

Paris and Île de France are famous for soups. There are dozens. To name a few: *purée* (or *potage*) *à la Crécy* (carrot) (see recipe), *potage aux primeurs* (spring vegetable) (see recipe); *potage cressonnière* (watercress and potato soup with cream); *potage bonne femme* (thick leek and potato soup); *potage* (or *purée*) *Soissonnais* (white haricot beans puréed in consommé); *gratinée* (thick onion soup) (see recipe).

Paris chefs invented many of the classic sauces and dishes: even *sauce Béarnaise*, invented around 1830 in a St Germain restaurant, Pavillon Henri Quatre, and therefore named for Henry IV who came from Béarn (see recipe); *sauce Bercy* (white wine, shallots, with rich beef stock for steak, fish *fumet* for fish) (see recipe) and *sole Duglère* (poached, with sauce of white wine, tomatoes, onions, herbs and cream – invented by a chef at one of Paris's first restaurants in the eighteenth century). Paris claims to have invented *matelote*, the stew of freshwater fish, which come from Île de France rivers.

Paris is a city of street markets. It is also a city of pâtisseries and they are so tempting that diets are forgotten as you enter. *Gâteau Saint-Honoré*, named for the patron-saint of pastry cooks, is made of little balls of *choux* pastry, filled with cream and ice. *Vol-au-vents* are filled with creamy rich things, whether savoury or sweet. *Gâteau Paris-Brest* (named after an early cycle race) is an éclair pastry ring filled with coffee cream; *gâteau Parisien* is sponge covered with meringue. Around the Madeleine in Paris are magnificent shops selling superb, very expensive food, from *brioche* to pâté and cakes. Fauchon is the greatest. Try to see this shop if only for its pâtés and bread. It caught fire a few years ago. When he heard, Denis Norden said: 'How terrible – but it must have smelt *delicious*!'

CHEESES

Brie is the premier cheese of this region. It came first from Meaux, when the town was in the Champagne. Now it is in Île de France. And the best brie is still *brie de Meaux fermier*, made on local farms. It is made from rennetted cow's milk and nearly all made in factories now. Some factory brie is not worthy of a cheese about which poems have been written. There are five other versions: Montereau (sharp), Mulen (sweeter, stronger smelling), Coulommiers (enriched with cream), Fougères (or Fougeru) and Grotte-paille.

Fontainebleau is a very light creamy cheese, rather tasteless, often eaten with sugar and cream. Triple-crème is better. Baguette Laonnaise is a very strong cheese from Laon.

9

CHAMPAGNE

Champagne is usually accused of stealing its culinary ideas from its neighbours, Île de France and Burgundy, which seems to be a good idea. In fact, it also uses ideas from Lorraine, Flanders, and its own Ardennes. With excellent home-grown ingredients it produces an amalgam of regional dishes which, if not inspired, are tasty and interesting.

Charcuterie is outstanding even for this area of France. If you like it, you need to do very little cooking. Troyes produces famous *andouillettes* (chitterling sausages) of pure pork and more rarely of mutton. They are usually grilled and served with mashed potatoes (see recipe). The ancient city also produces *langues fourrées* (tasty stuffed tongue). Delicious *andouillettes* come also from Bar-sur-Aube and Bar-sur-Seine, and charcuteries offer a range of many types of regional sausages, plus many from over the border in Alsace-Lorraine. White pudding (*Boudin blanc*) of Rethel is pleasant grilled gently in foil, then browned off.

Reims has a high reputation for any pork products, especially *jambon de Reims en croûte* (like a square vol-au-vent, with a thick slice of ham in puff pastry) and breaded ham knuckles. Pig's trotters are popular in the Champagne. If you intend to cook them, buy them ready-prepared from a charcuterie. A regional delicacy is *pied de porc à la Sainte Menehould* (grilled and breaded pig's trotters) (see recipe).

The Champagne is a region of thickly wooded hills. It includes the Ardennes and its streams, the vine-covered hills around Reims and the lakes and larger forests of the south-east which produce a variety of scenery and of good food. Wild boar, deer, hare and game birds still roam the Ardennes and its *jambon de sanglier* and *pâté de sanglier* (wild boar ham and pâté) are delicious. Beware if you have the naturalist's love of the thrush. Thrushes are made into pâté in the Ardennes and, unlike the Ardennes pâté you buy outside France, any *terrine à la Ardennaise* could well be made with thrush (*grive*). So ask. *Civet de lièvre* (jugged hare) is splendid but on holiday you won't want to go through the long business of preparing it. Try the bottles or jars offered in butchers, charcuteries or even supermarkets.

The rivers and lakes produce pike, perch and *sandre* (a cross between the two) and pike is used in one dish which the Champenoises claim as their own — *pain à la Reine* — a pike mousse or loaf made with potato and onion. Usually served hot with a superb crayfish sauce, I have seen it offered cold in shops and it makes a pleasant cold starter.

A problem with pike is that it is so bony. Not even French fishmongers are keen to bone it for you. If you can get it boned, the bones and head make a good fumet (fish stock). Boil 1 kilogramme of bones and trimmings for 30 minutes with a small onion finely diced, parsley, sprig of thyme, half a bay leaf, a few drops of lemon juice, 1 litre of water and 250ml of dry white wine. Strain.

Two dishes from neighbouring regions, slightly modified are *coq au vin de Bouzy* from Burgundy (Bouzy is the red wine of Champagne), and *potée Champenoise*, like *potée Lorraine* although a whole chicken is sometimes boiled with the rest.

Champagne claims *profiteroles*, very similar to éclairs, but so does the Île de France. If not original, cakes, flans and tarts are especially good in the pâtisseries of the Champagne. Do try *poires à la Champenoise* (pear flan).

CHEESES

Though boundary changes have put brie in Île de France, Champagne produces excellent cheeses. Chaource, soft, creamy, rich cheese, not too sharp, comes from a town near the Burgundy border. Fairly similar, but smelling mushroomy, is Ervy, from a village of that name, and Barberey (or *fromage de Troyes*) also has this smell. All these are best between June and November. Langres, soft, creamy, strong, shaped like a truncated cone, is splendid but rare outside Langres (available May-October). Another cheese of the same shape is Chaumont, a delightful strong, spicey, supple cheese made by small dairies and farms. We like carré de l'est, though factory made — a milder version of Maroilles.

WINES

'Do not let us talk about Champagne,' said Jacques Mercier years ago to Arthur. 'Let us drink it.' Since the monk Dom Pérignon of Hautvilliers abbey discovered, in the seventeenth century, the secret of controlling secondary fermentation in the bottle by adding a dosage of sugar and spirit, Champagne has remained the great sparkling wine of the world. Others have copied the *méthode Champenoise* or have sunk to the level of putting sparkle in wine by blowing gas through it, but none is in the same class as Champagne. And as we write, the very words *méthode Champenoise* applied to other wines is to be banned by the EEC.

Briefly, Champagne is made by blending grapes from different vineyards and sold under the name of the maker. The wine is made from three grape types – *Chardonnay* (white), *pinot noir* (black) and *meunier* grown mostly in the Marne valley. *Pinot noir* is blended into all Champagne except *blanc de blancs. Crémant* means that the wine fizzes less. Pink Champagne is made by leaving the still wine in contact with black grape skins long enough to be tinted. *Extra-brut* and *brut* wines are very slightly sugared, *sec* (dry) is given more sugar, *semi-sec* is quite sweet, *rich* or *doux* wines are very sweet. Vintage years are declared by Champagne producers only when wines are outstanding. They are naturally much dearer than NV (non-vintage) wines.

There are dozens of Champagne houses making their own wine. Most are in Reims and Epernay, but a number are based in Ay (including Bollinger) and villages around it, and in or around Châlons-sur-Marne.

The best known name is probably Moët-et-Chandon (you pronounce the 't' in Moët), a very reliable marque. Moët also owns Mercier (350m away) and the original cellar at Hautvilliers, so they call their very best vintages Dom Pérignon. It is very expensive and superb. Almost equally rare and expensive is Krug – heady, refreshing and delightful.

Champagnes do vary a lot in price, type and quality. Mercier, for instance is the lesser Champagne of Moët, but with a very nice flavour.

Some of the main Champagne houses are (comments refer to non-vintage): Heidsieck; Lanson (a good aperitif); Mumm; Laurent Perrier (lightish); Perrier Jouët (full, satisfying); Pol Roger (light and delightful); Alfred Rothschild (deserves to be better known); Taittinger (distinctive and very good); Veuve Cliquot (a widow who knows her own mind; one of our favourites).

Cellar visits are a must, but get a list before you go. They can be obtained, in Britain, from: The Champagne Bureau, Crusader House, 14 Pall Mall, London SW1Y 5LU. 01-839-1461; and in America, from: Irving, Smith, Kogan and Company, 220 East 42nd St, New York, 10017. Tel. 212-907-9380. Or, in Epernay, from: Comité Interprofessionel du Vin de Champagne, 5 rue Henri Martin, 51200 Epernay, Tel. (26) 54.47.20. Well known houses which accept casual visitors include: Moët-et-Chandon, 18 ave de Champagne, 51200 Epernay (26) 54.71.11; Mercier, 73 ave de Champagne, 51200 Epernay (26) 54.71.11 (every day – except shut on Sundays from 1 November to 31 March; G.M. Mumm, rue du Champ de Mars, 51100 Reims (26) 40.22.73 (Mon-Fri); Piper-Heidsieck, 51 boulevard Henri Vasnier, 51100 Reims (26) 85.01.84 (every day except weekends from 1 November to 31 March). Visiting hours at most houses are 9.30 a.m. to 12.00 a.m. and from 2.00 p.m. to 5.00 p.m.

The still, white wine of the Champagne is called Coteaux Champenois. It is strictly controlled, including the amount made, can be drunk as an alternative to white Burgundy, but tends to be pricey for what it is. A friend ordered Vin du Pays in a country auberge and found himself paying for a Coteaux!

The wine trade rates Bouzy, the best Champagne red wine, well below good Burgundy, but we find it excellent with heavier dishes and cheese. Not much is made, most is drunk locally. Rilly and Verzenay also produce reds.

Marc de Champagne is distilled from the leftovers of grapes after pressing. Once a poor man's brandy, it now has delusions of grandeur, served with sorbet, like a Calvados, mid-meal as a digestif.

10

LOIRE & WESTERN LOIRE

The lush valley of the Loire is fed from springs in the Massif Central which send the waters tumbling and bubbling down to this beautiful plain long known as the Garden of France. Here the French aristocrats besported themselves for 500 years indulging in all the pleasures of field, forest, table and bed. And despite the odd nuclear energy plant and the industrial growth of cities such as Le Mans and Orléans, it remains a superbly stocked larder where you can eat really well on local products without spending time on complicated dishes.

It is rightly proud of its fruit and nuts. Le Mans *reinette* apples have survived the French national marketing campaign for Golden Delicious. Raspberries, strawberries and blackberries are prolific in season, with Saumur as the main centre. Orléans produces quince (*coing*) and you can buy lovely quince jelly (*gelée de coing*), quince marmalade (*marmalade de coing*) and raspberry jelly (*gelée de framboise*). These are not usually spread on bread or toast but eaten with a spoon with sweet biscuits, cream or put in flans and tarts. A paste of quince and apple is called *cotignac*. Incidentally, bread spread with jam is usually called *tartine*. The jellies are especially delightful with *crémets* of Angers or Saumur (cream cheese mixed with white of eggs and served with cream) (see recipe).

Tours is best known for its plums and prunes and dishes made from them. Damson prunes (*gros damas de Tours*) are claimed to be the best in the world. Before nouvelle or moderne cuisines became fashionable and fruit was served with many meat dishes, French chefs despised the mixture of meat and fruit with one exception – *porc aux pruneaux* (see recipe). *Prunes fourrées* are plums stuffed with almond paste. You can buy the paste (*pâté d'amandes*).

Almonds

Tours also produces walnuts and they are used in salads and made into walnut oil to put on salads. Make a mixed dressing of walnut oil and red wine vinegar, which is delicious. Wine vinegar, white and red, is a speciality of Orléans. Pithiviers is the centre for almonds and they make a cake called 'pithiviers' of puff pastry with almonds and rum, traditionally bought after mass on Sunday as a lunch dessert (see recipe). Another local dessert which you can buy ready-made at a pâtisserie is savarin made in a ring of baba dough (like rum-baba), soaked in a rum syrup which includes cinnamon, coriander, aniseed and mace. The inside of the ring is often filled with fruit and cream – or it is served with crystallised fruit.

The game-rich marshes and forests of Sologne in the east have, oddly, produced a dessert served all over France – *tarte Tatin*, from the Hotel Tatin at Lamotte-Beuvron, a *Logis de France* which Michelin does not even recognise. It is an upside-down caramelised apple tart, delicious when well made, horrible when badly made or stale and heated up.

The Sologne is said to produce the best winged game in France. Two specialities are pheasant casserole (*faisan en barbouille*) and venison cutlets with *poivrade* sauce (*côtelettes de chevreuil poivrade*) – but that takes 5 hours to cook properly. Wild duck, hare, partridge and quail abound in season. So, alas, do lark. If you do not fancy eating wild songbirds, watch your pâtés in the Loire area. Chartres pâté can be of lark or partridge (*mauviette* or *perdreau*), Pithiviers pâté is usually lark in a pastry case (*pâté d'alouette*), Etampes and Blois produce lark pies and Gien thrush pâté (*pâté de grives* – eaten in most parts of France). Rabbit pâté is a speciality of Anjou, hare pâté of the Sologne.

Rillettes are made all over France but the best are from Le Mans and Tours. They are usually made of pork, but Le Mans adds goose to it and you can get rabbit. The meat is shredded, seasoned heavily, cooked, pounded and potted in its own fat. Buy it at the charcuterie. Serve on toast, using the fat instead of butter. *Rillauds* and *Rillons* are not pounded after cooking. You can also buy them in open tarts (*quiche Tourancelle*).

Market gardens of the Loire produce some of Europe's finest vegetables, which makes many modern recipes, using matchsticks of carrot as décor, seem out of place. Market gardens also produce excellent lettuce and other salad ingredients. Even cabbage is a delicacy. Asparagus – a thick white variety – is grown in the sand of the Loire banks, especially near Chambord. *Haricots verts* (green string beans) are picked young and small and are absolutely delicious. Boil them for 4 minutes only to keep them crisp and with full flavour. Out of season, do not despise the tinned version of *petits pois* (tiny peas cooked with lettuce and small onions). Broad beans (*fèvres*) are picked young, too. When they get a little older, the French remove the outer tough skin, which makes them into a different vegetable. Try the Poitou way – cooked, then dressed with butter and cream (called *mogettes*). Leeks of Touraine are often made into a simple leek sauce by stewing in butter, then adding Béchamel sauce to serve with the famous chicken of La Flèche. Bourges is another poultry area and duck come from Nantes. Mushrooms are grown extensively in caves unsuited to wine storage.

Fish is the mainstay of Loire and Lower Loire tables – shellfish from the Poitou coast, *anguilles* and *anguillettes* from the estuary. Freshwater pike, perch, sandre, shad and salmon come from the Loire, Cher, Loir, Loiret and the lakes and streams of Sologne. *Matelote à la marinière* is a stew of mixed boned freshwater fish.

Beurre blanc is served with freshwater fish, although we like it too with plaice, turbot or seabass (see recipe). Apart from salmon dishes, our favourite freshwater dish is hot pike mousse with crayfish sauce (*mousse de brochet au coulis d'écrevisses*) (see recipe). This is as good with cod, even better with salmon trout, which is less trouble to fillet, but dearer. Prawns can replace crayfish.

Salmon is often marinaded in red wine and cooked in a red wine *court-bouillon*, as in Basque cooking.

CHEESES

If you love strong goat's cheese, Sancerre has the best – *crottin de Chavignol* (matured, sharp-tasting with a rancid smell, and quite beautiful! Like a small flattened ball. *Crottin* means manure). Ste Maure, a long log with white rind, has a goaty smell, too. Chabichou is a tangy small cone-shaped goat's cheese, but get the *fermier* (farm) version, not the factory (best from May to February). Chabris and Mothe St Héray are both boxed like Camembert but taste quite different. Valençay and Livroux are nutty goat's cheeses made on farms (available May-February). Though factory made, Olivet bleu is a pleasant soft cow's milk cheese with a fruity taste. Olivet cendré, firm and supple, is cured and coated in ashes.

WINES

The main wines of the Loire from west to east are: Muscadet, the dry white once drunk only with fish but now rightly drunk more liberally as an aperitif or to accompany fish, poultry and starters such as light mousses. Drink it young (2-3 years old) for the fruitiest flavour, pay a little more for better wines (such as Galissonnière, Jannière, Gautronnières, Les Quatre Routes). 'Sur Lie' wine, bottled straight off the lees, makes wine even fruitier. Bourgueil, the red Touraine wine with body and fruity taste, which can be drunk quite young, rather despised by wine snobs until recently, is now quite fashionable. St Nicolas-de-Bourgueil produces some of the best wines. Vouvray, flowery, spicy wine with a long-lasting taste from a mixture of sand and gravel north of the Loire, can be dry, is more often *demi-sec* (sweetish). Good years improve up to 10 years; often made into sparkling wines, dry or sweet. Sancerre, one of our favourite white wines, fruity, fragrant, slightly smokey is delicious with fish, poultry or charcuterie. Pouilly Fumé, no relation to Burgundy's Pouilly Fuissé, smokier, fuller, is superb with charcuterie, chicken, duck and even game.

But all these have become fashionable, especially in Paris and are rather overpriced, except lesser Muscadet, which can be sharp, lacking fruit and not very nice.

There are lesser known alternatives. Gros Plant, made in the Muscadet area is fresh but rustic and at its worst like battery acid. Anjou produces good fragrant rosé wines. White wines are produced from the Chenin Blanc grape (called here 'Pineau de la Loire'), popular in the Loire. Wines leave your mouth dry and to our mind are not nearly equal to fruity Sauvignon whites, though a few, such as Savennières, are excellent. Saumur produces a very good rosé, and a fruity red Saumur-Champigny, fashionable 10 years ago. The dry and *demi-sec* white wines here are also made from Chenin and are made into perhaps the best sparkling wine outside Champagne. In 1811, Ackerman, an Alsatian, moved here and made the first wine ever made outside Champagne by the Champagne method. The company Ackerman-Laurance still make the wine at the Saumur suburb of St Hilaire-St Florent and you can visit and taste it. Also Muscadet and an excellent Touraine Sauvignon which we drink at home.

Look out for almost any Sauvignon de Touraine, but especially Vignoble de Corbillières. Montlouis, across the Loire from Vouvray, produces a drinkable dry white, acid when young, softer later. Touraine Amboise white and red are ordinary but good value. Jasnières is a pleasant sweet white. Chinon reds have a different flavour from Bourgueil but come mostly from the same grape Cabernet Franc and are as fruity, but seem lighter, and are usually cheaper.

Though not so smokey nor fruity as Sancerre, Quincy and Reuilly whites are cheaper and can be crisp and refreshing and easy to drink. Reuilly has some drinkable red, too.

11

BURGUNDY

In Dijon's Musée des Beaux-Arts, the old Ducal Palace, you can see still the awesome kitchen with six huge fireplaces where gargantuan banquets were cooked for Philip the Bold, John the Fearless and those other hard living, hard fighting, hard eating and drinking Dukes of Burgundy. 'Better a good meal than fine clothes' was the Burgundian motto. Cuisine and wine making are still Beaux Arts. Burgundians still eat lustily. Walk round the shops instead of supermarkets and you will see why.

From the lush meadows not only of Charolles but Morvan and the Nivernais comes the succulent beef of the white Charolais cattle, the best in France, though in our view not so superb as the Black Angus of Scotland and Canada. From the wooded hills of Morvan comes delicious game in season – tasty marcassin (young boar), woodcock, pheasants, venison and especially hare. Rivers provide trout, salmon, salmon trout, perch, pike, carp and eels. Above all, the streams of Morvan provide delicate freshwater crayfish. From Bresse, just across the border in Ain, come the best chickens in France, and possibly in Europe.

There are no longer enough of the traditional yellowish, dark-banded snails in vineyards or 'farms' to satisfy France's appetite for them, so many you see will have come from Eastern Europe.

Pork is the traditional meat of Burgundy. The pigs of the Morvan, fed on potatoes and dairy by-products, provide the delicious Morvan ham and dozens of local sausages and pâtés. Pork-fat bought from the butcher is used as a basis for cooking, like butter or oil in other areas.

The charcuterie of Burgundy rivals that of Alsace and Lorraine. If you don't want to do much cooking, you can live for days on delicacies from the charcuterie. There's the Morvan ham eaten raw and *jambon persillé* (cold ham boiled with pigs trotters in white wine, crushed, layered with parsley and set in jelly of its stock). There is an array of cooked sausages, cooked chicken and game. Smoked boar in jelly is delicious. A delightful supper dish is *boeuf à la mode* cold in its own jelly (top rump marinaded then braised in red wine with carrots, onions and calves foot jelly; also served hot in restaurants).

Most charcuteries sell *gougère*, a tasty delicate cheese ring of puff pastry (*choux*), served cold or hot, but these are easy to make (see recipe). Also *fouée*, a cream and bacon flan of flaky pastry, topped with walnut oil, which is nicer hot.

Some charcuteries sell escargots (snails) ready stuffed with garlic, shallots and parsley butter. You simply put them in a hot oven until the butter sizzles. Incidentally, if you pluck snails from the hedgerows, remember that you must 'park' the snails for several days, feeding them only on lettuce, thyme and water to clear them of any poison. Then boil them to detach them from their shells, cook them in *court-bouillon*, then put them back in their shells for stuffing. We would rather pay for them.

If you like chitterling sausages, *andouillettes* (which we don't), choose between versions from Chablis, Arnay-le-Duc, Clamecy and Macon. They are grilled and served with Dijon mustard. Sausages are often baked in pastry and served with red-wine sauce.

Burgundians use marinades a lot for meat, game and fowl. Usually they marinade meat in red wine with sliced carrot, onion, salt, pepper, diced celery, parsley, bay leaf and thyme (the usual method) but *marc* (brandy distilled from grape residue) replaces wine as marinade in old traditional recipes for game and *boeuf bourguignon* (see recipe).

Morvan grows a variety of mushrooms, especially *morilles*, with a lovely earthy flavour. These cooked with little white onions and fried strips of bacon are the traditional garnish to meats and fowl. With traditional red wine sauce and carrots it becomes *meurette*. A simple dish is poached eggs *en meurette* (see recipe).

Fishmongers sell coarse fish from the River Saône in season (pike, small carp, tench, eel, perch). These are cooked two ways — as pouchouse, simmered in a good white wine, such as Macon, with a clove of garlic and cream added at the end. A delightful delicate dish. Or as a *matelote*, in red wine. You make a fish *fumet* by boiling bones, head and trimmings from the fish with a chopped onion, mushroom

Eel

stalks and a *bouquet garni* of thyme, parsley and bay in a litre of red wine, strain, boil down by half, then stir in 2½ tablespoons (40g) of kneaded butter (mixed to a paste with 50g of flour). Cut freshwater fish in chunks, simmer it in the *fumet* with browned bacon strips, chopped carrots, crushed garlic. Some chefs add a small glass of *marc*. Serve with bread fried in butter, rubbed with garlic. A short cut is to discard the heads and cook fish and the rest in wine.

Bresse chickens *are* delicious (see recipe). Hand-plucked, they have a distinguishing ruff of feathers and metal ring. Imported from Ain in large quantities into Burgundy, they are usually poached jointed in white wine and cream, sometimes with puréed crayfish tails and butter. Crayfish (*écrevisses*) from Morvan rivers are cooked in a white wine *court-bouillon* (*à la nage*).

In Dijon very young chickens (*poussin*) are roasted painted all over with mustard (see recipe). For *Coq au Vin*, the great Burgundian dish, a young chicken should be used, not a tough old boiler (see recipe). Posher restaurants cook it in Chambertin (Gevrey, no doubt). And the traditional way to make *boeuf Bourguignon* is to leave the meat (topside, sirloin or rump) in a joint – not to cut it in cubes (see recipe).

Burgundian cooking is definitely not for people worried about weight, cholesterol or fibre diets. Even the splendid vegetables (cabbages, turnips, spinach, asparagus, marrow, beet) are cooked or served in cream, so are mushrooms. Crème de Cassis, the delicious blackcurrant liqueur mixed with cold white wine to make the refreshing aperitif Kir, is often used for sauces with pork or served with the meat in tartlets. But salads for dieters are excellent – lambs' lettuce (*mâche*), celery leaves, curly lettuce (served with garlic and bacon strips), endive, purple roquette. *Rapée* potatoes as cooked by Morvan farmers, are *not* for slimmers. You grate 1kg of potatoes, mix 300ml of cream with three eggs, grated cheese (gruyère) and garlic, mix this with the potatoes, put in a buttered dish, dot with butter and put in a medium oven for about an hour.

Blackcurrants, cherries and pears are the fruit used mostly in tarts. You can buy the sweet version of *rigodan* (brioche nut cake) in pâtisseries. It is splendid but not worth the trouble of making. They often sell *tourte charolaise* (tart filled with pears in creamy custard). Dijon's great *pain d'épice* is spiced honey gingerbread.

CHEESES

Best known local cheese is Epoisses – soft, tangy, slightly acid, from cow's milk, flavoured sometimes with black pepper, fennel, white wine or *marc*. Orange-red rind. Eaten fresh in summer, ripe November-June. Aisy-cendré is similar but covered in wood ashes in which it is stored.

Other cheeses include: Cow's milk – Citeaux (from the monastery of Citeaux, tangy, fruity flat disc with yellow rind and available June-November); Laumes (rare, made in farms. Strong, spicy, brown rind from washing in coffee. November-July); Saint Florentin (soft, triple-cream piquant factory cheese. White inside, yellow out, best when creamy, June-November); Soumaintrain (popular strong, soft, yellow cheese with golden crust. Good with red wine. November-July).

Goat's cheeses: Charolais (small log bluish rind, farm made, nutty. Best June-November); Chevretons de Macon (eaten young and creamy with sugar. Later firm and nutty, best May-September); Claquebitou (tastes of herbs and garlic. June-October); Vézelay (strong, from Morvan).

WINES

Most Frenchmen believe that Burgundy red wines are the world's best, ahead even of Bordeaux and have persuaded most of the world to believe the same. Hence spiralling prices, bid by American, Japanese and some German importers. The best Grand Cru wines and Premier Cru are now beyond the pockets of most people including the French. Happily, if you can forget the '74 Richebourg which Uncle George served you once, or that sublime Corton-Charlemagne white which a business acquaintance bought to impress you, you can enjoy some highly-drinkable lesser, cheaper wines with an Appellation Contrôlée label.

Wine production is strictly controlled, the system of classifying wine too complicated to describe here. You will find the lot in Serena Sutcliffe's paperback *The Wines of France* (Futura).

At the lower end are Bourgogne Grand Ordinaire, Bourgogne, Bourgogne Passetoutgrains (blend of Pinot Noir grapes, used in Burgundy, and Gamay, used in Beaujolais), Bourgogne Aligoté white wine (named after a grape and used with Crème de Cassis – blackcurrant liqueur – to make the aperitif Kir). Then come appellations such as Beaujolais Villages, Macon, Côte de Beaune Villages, Côte-de-Nuits Villages. Then there are village names like Gevrey-Chambertin, Fleurie, Meursault, Chassagne Montrachet. Second from the top are Premier Cru wines. Top are Grand Cru.

Some villages have added the name of their best vineyard to give them prestige. Gevrey became Gevrey-Chambertin and the wines vary in quality, whilst Le Chambertin and Clos de Bèze are nectar and very pricey indeed. Nuits added 'St Georges', Chambolle added 'Mussigny'. Le Mussigny itself is another superb, expensive wine.

Apart from the white wines Chablis and Pouilly Fuissé, all the Grand and Premier Crus are on the Côte d'Or (Côte de Nuits – Dijon to Corgoloin, and Côte de Beaune – southward to Santenay). The N74 is the great wine road.

But Côte Chalonnais further south has some rewarding and cheaper wines. Rully – both white and red – are hugely improved, thanks largely to Jean-Francois Delorme (look for his Varot, La Chaume and Domaine de la Renarde wines). Also Jean Coulon's white Blanc Grésigny. Reds are fruity and nutty. Whites are dry, fruity and rather acidic when young. You are supposed to drink them within 3 years but we also like the older wines – smoother with a little less fruit – and sometimes cheaper! Much white is made into 'Sparkling Burgundy'. Givry – mostly red, fruity, lightish; good for lunch. Try Clos de Cellier aux Moines and Clos St Pierre. Mercurey – solid red which goes, like Beaune, with Burgundian dishes. Better 4 to 5 years old but not much longer. Montagny – dry white, heavier than Rully, can be coarse. Try wines of Louis Latour and Buxy Co-operative. Côte Maconnaise, further south, makes mostly Macon dry white from Chardonnay grape; but one of the best known is the red Macon made mostly from Gamay grapes, like Beaujolais. We all know Pouilly Fuissé, the great dry white, but it is overpriced because of its popularity in America and some cheaper wines are not up to standard.

Cheaper and a fair alternative are Pouilly-Loché and Pouilly-Vinzelles, not quite so smooth. They are best about 3 to 5 years old. St Véran white can be drunk when 2 years old.

Chablis Premier Cru should not be drunk until at least 4

years old, and Grand Cru should be older. Some French drink them too young, which annoys Burgundians.

Until serious controls were established, a lot of Nuits St Georges sold abroad was not old enough. Some cheaper wines in the area will surprise you. Don't drink them too young. Negociants you can trust are F. Chauvenet, J. Faiveley, Morin, Liger-Belair. From the hills behind Nuits come the cheaper good-value wines Bourgogne Hautes-Côtes de Nuits. Corgoloin has a good Côtes de Nuits Village wine, Clos des Langres.

Excellent value on Côte de Beaune is red Monthélie – light, fragrant, brilliant red, maturing nicely in 3 to 4 years. It is like a lesser, cheaper Volnay. So are Auxey-Duresses reds. The whites have a delightful bouquet and with a little more flavour could rival Meursault – at half the price. Two more great value wines are St Romain dry white, delicious as an aperitif when young, or its red (look for Roland Thévenin wines) and red St Aubin.

12

RHÔNE (LYONNAIS, ARDÈCHE, BRESSE, NORTH RHÔNE VALLEY)

Small wonder that the Lyonnais is the fountain-head of classical French cooking. It draws its ingredients from a gastronomic larder – Bresse, La Dombe, Forez, Beaujolais and the Rhône valley.

Nouvelle cuisine was started here, too, by Fernand Point at La Pyramide at Vienne, 30 kilometres south of Lyon. A recent return reminded Arthur just how far from Pyramide cuisine nouvelle has gone in eccentric directions since. And Paul Bocuse has his restaurant at Collonges – once High Priest of Nouvelle, accused of serving raw food as *haute cuisine*, now a law unto himself who blessedly served Arthur with a hillock of young French beans recently. Perhaps it was a surfeit of the massive portions of solid bourgeois dishes popular in this whole area which drove locals to seek meals of delicate, unsatisfying trifles.

From Bresse come *poulets de Bresse*, tender white chickens fed on maize and buckwheat, and allowed to roam free for 7 months, the only poultry with an Appellation Contrôlée and a red badge and metal ring to prove it. They are superb. From Lyon comes the expensive *poulet demi-deuil* (the chicken's breast spiked with truffles, stuffed with sausage, poached and served with cream sauce) and *poulet Céléstine* (see recipe); and from Bresse itself *poularde à la Nantua* (with crayfish sauce) (see recipe); but Bresse chicken is superb simply roasted in butter. Corn makes the livers soft and yellow (*foies blonds de volaille*).

From Beaujolais comes Charolais beef. From the hilly forests of Forez westward comes game, and inevitably pâtés and terrines abound in charcuteries. And the shops of the Ardèche are full of treasures to make superb meals – *jambonnettes* (boned ham stuffed with fresh pork meat), *cayettes* (rissoles of pork, spinach and cabbage), *escargots farcis* (snails stuffed with parsley butter), *dindonneau farci aux marrons* (cold boned turkey stuffed with chestnuts, sold in slices), *pâté de canard Lucullus* (truffled pâté of duck), *poulet en vessie* (chicken sausages). True, you can buy most of these in Lyon's charcuteries, too, imported from Ardèche. Lyon's most famous sausage is *saucisson de Lyon* (or *Jésus de Lyon*), enormous, made of ham, fresh pork and liver, eaten raw as *hors d'oeuvre*. Cervelas sausage (like saveloy) is poached for 30 minutes, served hot. Sausages are also baked whole in a brioche casing (sold in charcuteries – *saucisson en brioche* – the ultimate toad-in-the-hole, served hot or cold).

The lovely Ardèche river is rich in fish, but so are the other rivers of this area – the Rhône, Saône and Loire, and the waterways of Dombes, north-east of Lyon, which produces, too, woodcock, pigeon, snails and frogs legs.

The Rhône valley claims to have invented *quenelles* – little fish soufflés made by mashing fish, blending it with cream and egg into finger shapes and poaching them until they swell. *Quenelles de brochet* (pike *quenelles*, served with crayfish sauce) were the originals (see recipe). But good charcuteries vie with each other to produce inventive versions, with fillings of mussels, shrimps, salmon, crayfish, mushrooms in cream sauce, even pistachio nuts, or a mixture. Don't buy supermarket versions – they often taste starchy and are heavy. Charcuteries and pâtisseries in this whole area are a joy to see, and so are stalls in local markets, which abound.

The Rhône valley is covered in vines, fruit trees and Roman ruins. Fruit includes cherries, apricots, peaches,

Apricots

pears, plums and apples. You can buy (or make) *tourte Charolaise* – tart filled with pears in creamy custard. *Pralines* (sugar coated roasted almonds – beware of tooth fillings!) from Montargis are crushed to use in a superb dessert *gâteau Lyonnais* (includes pears and apricots) (see recipe). *Tendresses* are rum-flavoured nougat sweets in meringue casing. And chestnuts and chestnut *purée* are used for delicious desserts, too (*flan aux marrons*) (see recipe). *Marrons glacés* are expensive even here. Montelimar makes lovely nougat, served sometimes as a dessert.

CHEESES

Bleu de Bresse is a creamy blue cheese with mild taste (factory made). Favourite local cheese is Mont d'Or, soft, mild, delicate, in large thin rounds. Originally of goat's milk, it is now made of cow's milk. Picoden, from Montelimar, is a pleasant goats' cheese. Bressan is a firm, fruity goats' cheese. Brique (or cabrion) du Forez is a splendid nutty cheese from Forez farms, with white and blue rind (best June-November). Chevrets, Chevretons, Beaujolais, Maconnais, *boutons de culottes* are all soft fresh goats' cheeses eaten as dessert with sugar or fruit.

WINES

From Beaujolais to the great wines of Hermitage, you have a superb choice. The best have risen in price as former Burgundy drinkers have changed their habits to suit their pockets, but there are plenty of drinkable and good wines to suit you and your bank manager. We have not included here the southern Côtes du Rhône wines such as Châteauneuf du Pape; and Vaucluse wine such as Gigondas.

There are nine Beaujolais *crus* (top growths), all with definite characteristics. Wines called Beaujolais Villages which come from any of 40 communes include wines of excellent value. 'Supérieur' means stronger, not better. Some white is made but the nine *crus* are red: Moulin-à-Vent is deep-coloured and smooth. Though most Beaujolais is drunk young, if you find an old Moulin it will taste superb. Morgon wine is strong, has an earthy taste and also keeps well. St Amour is a fruity, delicate wine from a small area. Juliénas, purply in colour, is fruity when young but full. Chénas is rare, excellent but a bit rougher than Moulin. Fleurie is our favourite – fruity, charming, soft, nice young, keeps well. Chiroubles is a light wine which we prefer young. Brouilly and Côte de Brouilly produce lovely fruity, refreshing, mouth-filling wines becoming fashionable in Paris. Better after 3 years old.

Some pleasant Gamay wines come from the Côtes de Forez. Drink them young and cold – not iced. When you reach the Côtes du Rhône you have a superb choice. Around Tain are the deep red wines of Hermitage, delightful, as long lasting as the great clarets and inevitably very pricey as the soil sometimes gets washed down the steep slope and has to be carried back! White Hermitage, too, is full, nutty and keeps well. Crozes-Hermitage wines do not last so long, are not quite in Hermitage class and are cheaper. Look for Jaboulet wines – white and red. Our favourite substitute for Hermitage is St Joseph (known to our Victorian ancestors as Mauves) across the Rhône river. The red wines are strong and have an earthy, natural taste. Do try them. The French drink them too young. If you can find a 1979, it will be worth its money. White St Joseph wines can become full and rich-tasting after 3 or 4 years.

Cornas red wine can be rough when young and becomes excellent from 5 years old. Local red wines of the Côte Rotie are cheapish and good for daily drinking and from the Ardèche look for the Coteaux de l'Ardèche wines made from Gamay grape – much underrated and good value. The VDQS red wines Côtes de Viverais are made to be drunk young.

Try Condrieu white as a cheaper alternative to Chablis or Pouilly Fuissé. When young, it seems to taste of fruit blossom. Georges Vernay and Delas Frères make good wines.

St Péray is usually sparkling, made by *Champagne méthode* – but just a fruity refreshing aperitif – *not* Champagne!

13

POITOU-CHARENTES

Charentes chefs need no frills. Some of France's richest lands give superb butter, fine beef, salt-grazed lamb from south of La Rochelle, lovely vegetables and fruit, including Niort's outstanding cauliflowers and Charentais melons. Fish, too – white fish from La Rochelle, one of Europe's biggest fishing ports, oysters from Marennes, mussels from the farms of Boyardville off the Isle of Oléron, *lampreys* (eels) from estuaries, trout and *anguilles* (more eels) from the rivers, and pork from around Angoulême. Free-range chickens and ducks are still raised on farms, and eggs from farms or markets are delicious. The Charente river, once used for taking wine and brandy to the seaports, now wanders through lush *prés* – meadows flooded in winter, dotted in summer with cows which produce superb cream and butter rivalling the butter of Normandy as the best in France. So cooking is based on butter, laced with cream, wine and often flamed in that other well known local product, cognac. Most cuisine is what the French call 'honest and direct', so finding the best markets is more important than having a complicated recipe book.

We have found splendid sea-bass in La Rochelle fish market. It is usually called 'bar' around here, 'loup de mer' in some other parts of France. A favourite local recipe is *bar farci* (baked, stuffed with egg, spinach and herbs). But we find this delicately-flavoured fish superb poached in wine (see recipe). Sea-bass is quite a big fish, but if you do not finish it hot, it is delicious served cold with mayonnaise, garlic mayonnaise, or vinaigrette dressing with herbs. We think tartare sauce too strong for it. *Mouclade Charentaise* (or *Rochelaise*) is mussels in cream similar to the Brittany dish (see recipe) but with ¼ teaspoon of curry powder and ¼

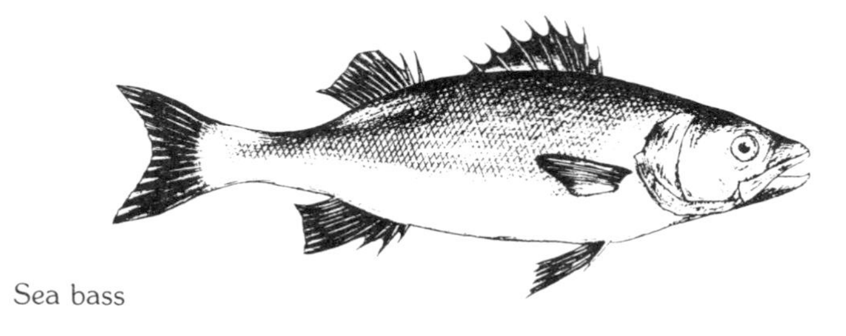

Sea bass

teaspoon of mustard added for 1 litre of mussels. *Moules Rochelaises* usually means mussels stuffed with herb butter and grilled brown. In Charente mussels are cooked in Pineau – a local aperitif made from young wine and brandy (*Moules au Pineau des Charentes*) (see recipe). Mussels are also served in omelettes.

Marais Poitevin, the mysterious land of drained marshes where people and animals – even sheep and goats – travel in flat-bottomed *plattes* (poled punts) provides some fine freshwater fish, including trout (*truite à la Poitevine*) (see recipe) and little eels, made into *bouilleture d'anguilles* (stewed in red wine) (see recipe).

Charentes vegetables are made into some unusual dishes. *Mojettes à la crème* (creamed haricot beans) take a while to cook but are a rewarding change from potatoes with roast meat, fowl or even stews (see recipe). *Fas* (or *farée*) *de Poitou* is a sort of loaf of green vegetables served cold or hot as a starter or as a vegetable with grills. It is delicious and very useful as it keeps in fridge or freezer (see recipe).

Charentes meadow-grazed veal and veal kidneys are succulent and tastier than white veal produced in torture chambers (see recipe).

Eggs are served poached on fried bread with kidneys in a meat sauce (*oeufs pochés a l'Huguenot*), an unnecessary embellishment when eggs are free-range and fresh.

Chestnuts, almonds and walnuts are grown in south Poitou. Salads are often dressed with walnut oil and wine vinegar. Macaroons are made in several places; *Macarons de Niort* are much prized.

CHEESES

Despite the superb Charentes butter (or because of it) little good cow's milk cheese is made. Aunis, a triangular sheep's milk cheese, is delicious. Chabichou, carré de St Cyr and especially Mothe-Sainte-Héray are good goats' cheeses.

WINES

Though there has been a resurgence of wine-making in Northern Poitou near the Loire area, this is mainly not table wine country. The thin acidic wine of Charentes is distilled into cognac. Because the Dutch objected to shipping costs for this inferior wine during the Renaissance, it was distilled to reduce weight and called Brandewijn (burnt wine) – instant wine, just add water. Brandies from different districts vary greatly. In order of importance, districts are Grande Champagne and Petite Champagne (both with very chalky soil, south of the town of Cognac), Borderies, Fins Bois, Bons Bois, and Bois Ordinaires (which stretches as far as La Rochelle and the isles of Oléron and Ré). Words like 'Napoléon' and 'paradis' do not signify a standard or grade but are in the eye of the bottler and palate of the drinker. Nor is VSOP a grade, though it usually means an older liqueur-quality brandy.

The wine is distilled by the small growers, then matured in old Limousin oak casks and blended by the Cognac houses such as Courvoisier, Rémy-Martin, and Hennessy. Hennessy has the world's largest reserves of old brandy and is the most rewarding house to visit. You can see a film of brandy production, a museum with old instruments and barrels, then cross the Charente river by a little ferry to see millions of gallons maturing in 30,000 casks in the *chaises* (warehouses) of La Faïencerie. The tour is conducted in English (visits Monday to Friday 8.30 to 11.00 a.m. and 1.45 to 4.30 p.m. James Hennessy and Co, 1 rue de la Richonne, 16100 Cognac. Tel: (45) 82.52.22).

Pineau, the local aperitif used much in cooking, is made from a blend of young local wine and Cognac, white or rosé, and is delicious. They say that it was discovered by accident when a drunken local tipped new wine into a cask still containing brandy.

Local Champerlé Charente white table wine is rather tart. Some red, white and rosé wines made in Haute Poitou have a VDQS appellation, using Chardonnay and Sauvignon grapes for whites, Pinot Noir, Cabernet and Gamay for reds. Most people here drink Loire wines but look out for crispy, dry Sauvignon from the Cave Co-operative of Haute-Poitou.

14

PÉRIGORD, QUERCY & ROUERGUE

Gone are the days when cuisine *à la Périgourdine* meant truffles with everything and how shall we serve the *foie gras* today? Truffles, the 'black diamond' fungus snuffled from beneath oak trees by gourmet-dogs from November to March and canned to be put in soup, sauces, stuffings, omelettes and pâtés the rest of the year, are now for the rich. And even if you can stomach the idea of eating the livers of force-fed geese or ducks your bank manager may insist that at current prices fresh *foie gras* and *pâté de foie gras* are for birthdays and special celebrations only.

Never mind. The charcuteries and pâtisseries of Périgord and Quercy are packed with treasures in pastry, cans and jars. *Confit* of duck and goose are the greatest delicacies – wing or leg of the birds preserved in their own fat. They are used for many dishes but a simple, delicious way to cook them is to melt the fat from around them and fry them gently until a golden crust forms. Sometimes a handful of sorrel leaves are added. The fat left in the pan is used to fry sliced potatoes to eat with the *confit*. Counter the richness with a Périgourdine salad – green salad, including dandelion leaves if you like their sharp flavour, curly endive, green beans or anything else you fancy, like cooked asparagus, cooked globe artichoke hearts, but always with chopped walnuts and

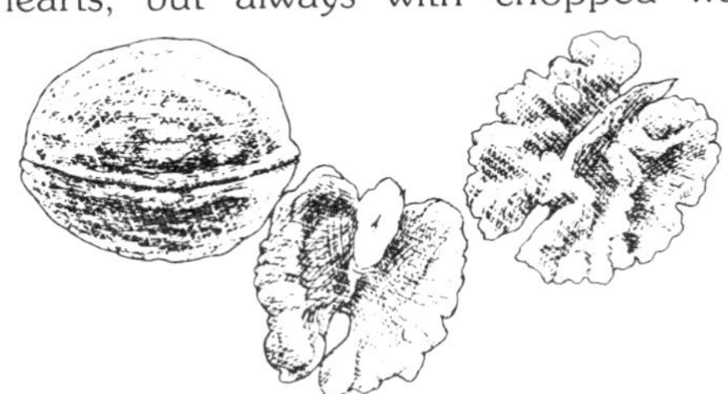

Walnuts

walnut oil mixed with wine vinegar. This is a great area for walnuts. When a young man took over his first farm he would plant walnut trees for his grandchildren.

Goose and duck fat are used for cooking in place of butter, lard or oil. You can buy it by weight in the butchers or in pots at other shops. Buying *confit* or pâté in a tin in this area does not mean that it is mass-produced in a factory. Boucheries, charcuteries, even restaurants and housewives do their own canning in season. Pâtés often contain small specks of truffle, cutaways from making other dishes but beware of very cheap 'truffled' pâtés – a black fungus (*trompettes de la mort*) is sometimes cheatingly substituted, and it neither has the right flavour nor does it enhance the flavours of other ingredients as truffles do so miraculously. If you do decide to splash out on tinned truffles, cook them *en croûte* (in pastry) with a little raw *foie gras* (not pâté) – *truffes en chaussons* (see recipe), or in an omelette (see recipe). If you have a good log fire, they are superb cooked in embers. Season with salt, pepper and spices, sprinkle with brandy. Wrap each truffle in fat off a rasher of bacon then in foil tightly. Put them in a metal dish in the ashes and embers and cover with ashes and embers for about 40 minutes. Canned truffles are usually steeped in brandy or Madeira wine, and this liquid, called truffle juice, is used in many dishes.

Cèpes, round-capped fleshy fungus, a regional speciality, are canned for out of season. In Sarlat, the old market town which was once an English headquarters in the Hundred Years' War, *cèpes* are served in *verjus*, acidic juice of unripe grapes used since mediaeval days as an alternative to vinegar. A few drops are put on another delicious fungus, *oranges de César*, which you grill for 4 minutes, then paint with walnut oil. *Rosés des prés*, delicate pinkish meadow mushrooms you can buy in markets, are cooked in goose fat with sliced potatoes, chopped parsley and garlic. Very nice.

Game tends to be domesticated, with boar kept in pens on farms and pheasant carefully reared, so *pâté de sanglier* (boar), *de marcassin* (young boar) and *de faisan* (pheasant) abound in charcuteries and at markets. *Quercy boudin blanc* is soft sausage of chicken and veal. You can often buy cooked *cou d'oie farci* (stuffed goose neck) to be served cold, cut like a sausage in slices. The old saying was: 'With a neck of goose, a loaf of bread and bottle of wine, you can invite your neighbour to a feast.' *Rillettes* are made with shredded goose left over from making *confit*. They are pounded with goose fat and eaten on bread – no butter needed!

Sarlat's Saturday market is renowned and Périgueux has one of the finest markets in France, but every little town has a market worth attending. In St Céré, one of our favourite little towns in France, where a little river runs alongside the square, you can buy in the Saturday market locally-tinned and bottled *confit*, pâtés, walnuts, greengages, cherries, plums, apricots, fresh or bottled in *eau de vie* to give you a drink and a dessert, fish from the River Dordogne nearby, fresh *foie gras* and magnificent free-range poultry. Turkeys are particularly delightful. Buy a big boiling fowl or a piece of bacon or salt pork and when you boil it make *miques* to go with it – traditional local dumplings. We have given the simple recipe from Sarlat, though in farmhouses they make them with bakers' yeast and used to put them under the bed covers to rise!

People here love soup so much that instead of asking if dinner is ready, they say: 'Have you made the soup?' Most are thick soups like stews. A good family stand-by is *sobronade*. Cut fresh pork and salt pork or ham into large dice and add haricot beans, leeks, celery, carrots, any other root vegetables, stock or water, salt and pepper, simmer indefinitely. As with *cassoulet* (see recipe) the beans make it thick. Keep it on the stove to heat up.

Among simple specialities are *les merveilles* – fritters eaten hot or cold and both ways when we are eating pancakes on Shrove Tuesday (Mardi Gras) (see recipe). Try also *cajasse sarladaise* (rum flavoured cake). Tins of *purée de marrons au naturel* (chestnut cream without sugar) are excellent for making stuffings or desserts (see recipe).

CHEESES

The Rouergue makes Arthur's favourite cheese – Roquefort, so expensive that locals save it for great occasions. The ewe's milk to make it comes from many regions, especially the High Pyrenees, but the cheese is matured for at least 3 months in the natural caves of Rouergue where an underground lake gives high humidity and temperature stays around 8°C (46°F). The blue parts come from mouldy breadcrumbs in alternate layers with cheese during maturing. Matured in these caves since 1411, genuine Roquefort carries a blue label. Beware of imitations.

Other cheeses are: bleu de Quercy (or bleu de Causses) – cow's milk, firm, blue cheese, much cheaper than Roquefort; best from October to February, but pleasant all year. Cabecou de Rocamadour or Livernon – soft nutty goats' cheese made on farms, best June to November. Wrapped in leaves, matured in crocks, Rocamadour becomes soft, strong, smelly, very tasty and is then called Picadou.

WINES

Bergerac is the nearest wine district to Bordeaux and in the past its wines once rivalled claret. Foreigners are drinking them again and so are northern French people. Bergerac reds are fruity and fairly soft, with Pécharmant most favoured. Try Château de Tiregand, produced by the Comte and Comtesse de St Exupéry, cousins of the airman-poet. Montravel, once producing sweet wine, now has also crisp, dry white wine which is excellent value. Monbazillac produces sweet wine which has improved enormously in recent years; not in true Sauternes class (though it was often mixed with Sauternes in the bad old days), it can be fragrant and luscious when allowed to age. Drink it with fruit or cheese. The best comes from Château Monbazillac, produced by a co-operative. Bergerac Rouges and Côtes de Bergerac rouge are fruity and not unlike Bordeaux's lesser wines from Blaye and Bourg. At Château de la Jaubertie at Colombier an Englishman, Nick Ryman, produces pleasant reds, superb dry white Bergerac, with a nice smell and delicate taste, one of the best Bergeracs.

Marmandais wines are produced mostly from similar grapes to Bordeaux and are often good value (try wines of the co-op at Cocumont – 'cuckold mount'). Wines of Côtes de Buzet have improved enormously since an expert from Lafite-Rothschild took over. Reds are aged in wood and are delightful after another 3 years in the bottle. As with Bordeaux, the French drink them too young.

They drink Cahors too young, too. Most of it goes on improving in the bottle for at least 10 years. The British always appreciated the dark, red strong wine of Cahors, but the French used most of it to give a bit of kick and colour to Bordeaux. Now it is more carefully made, is fashionable in Paris, and is dearer, but still excellent value. Superb with roast beef or strong game. Wines vary much and you get what you pay for. Dearer wines like Clos de la Coutale are fruity, smooth and full flavoured. Try Château de Cayrou, Clos de Gamot and Comte André de Monpézat. Château de Haute-Serre is fruity but lighter.

A liqueur (usually drunk as an aperitif) is made from chestnuts. Called Liqueur de Châtaigne, it is nicer than it sounds.

15

MASSIF CENTRAL (LIMOUSIN, AUVERGNE, BOURBONNAIS)

From the rich green rolling landscape of Limousin comes succulent beef, superb tasty wild mushrooms (*cèpes*, *chanterelles*, *morilles*), farmyard chickens, pigs and geese, with sophisticated dishes served perhaps on delicate Limoges porcelain. On the rugged volcanic plateau of Auvergne, where farming is hard and farmers hardy, you do not find much finesse or sophistication. Meals are hearty, wholesome, pleasant and peasant, with pork, potatoes and cabbage as base.

In north Auvergne they grow beets and lentils, too, and fruit – peaches, apricots, apples, pears, many of which go to Clermont Ferrand to make crystallised fruit. Strawberries and almonds are grown and are excellent in season.

Further south, milch cows graze the pastures producing delicious Auvergnat cheeses, also tasty field veal (see recipe).

In the mountains sweet lamb is produced, especially from Vassivieras. Nothing is wasted. *Tripoux* are a delicacy – sheep's trotters and calf's tripe simmered for hours. Lamb is often boned, with garlic put under the skin, and braised in wine with herbs and vegetables, then served with red beans and small onions.

Auvergne charcuterie is renowned all over France. Each village seems to produce its own varieties of sausages and pâtés. Mountain cured ham, served raw, is chewier than Bayonne, Parma or Ardennes ham but has a superb flavour. Ussel and St Mathieu hams are tender. We like especially the Auvergne *fricandeau*. Here it is not braised topside of veal, as elsewhere in France, but a delicious pork pâté wrapped in sheets of salt pork. *Friands de Saint Flour*, little sausage-meat pâtés wrapped in leaves or pastry are delicious. Try also *tourte à viande*, pork and veal pasties which you can eat hot or cold. Air dried sausages, pork liver pâtés, black pudding with chestnuts, stuffed pigs' trotters all abound in the shops. Uncooked sausages are bought to cook with lentils in stock. Brioude is known for salmon. You can buy jars of Ussel jellied eels. Freshwater fish is excellent, although most trout now comes from farms.

The most popular peasant dish of Auvergne, a stew called *potée Auvergnate*, has different versions in each district, but the basics are salt pork, cabbage, potatoes and sausages (see recipe).

There are dozens of potato dishes, many called *aligot*, *alicot* or *aligout*, and mostly delicious. Most popular is *trouffade* (or *truffade*). It can be made of mashed potatoes, mixed with *tomme* cheese, topped with grated cheese and butter, then grilled. Another way is to slice potatoes thinly, fry in lard with chopped bacon and garlic, and add grated cheese at the last moment. Make a simple *aligot* for four by boiling 1 kg of potatoes with garlic, salt, pepper, mashing them with 100 g of butter and 500 ml of milk, then stirring in very quickly 400 g of diced *tomme* cheese. Serve with sausages, poached, then browned under the grill. In the Auvergne and Bourbonnais a pâté is made of potatoes and cream in flaky pastry (see recipe). In Limousin, belly of pork is included and it is called *pâté Creusois* (see recipe). Both make a pleasant supper.

Limousin borders on Périgord and that area produces geese, *foie gras*, those superb mushrooms and excellent pork. *Carré de porc à la Limousine* is roast pork served with braised red cabbage and chestnuts (see recipe). In Limousin they follow the Périgordian way with soup. They 'faire chabrot' by leaving a spoonful in the bowl, pouring in a glass of red wine and drinking it.

Pastries are excellent in the whole Massif Central. Cream cornets (*cornet*) come from around Murat; *bourroilles* from Aurillac are heavy sweet buckwheat pancakes, *picoussel* are buckwheat cakes filled with plums and herbs, and *échaude* is a poached brown pastry square. Clermont-Ferrand has many specialities, including *angélique*, *flagnarde* (a jam flan or pancake), and *milliard*, a cherry tart (beware – the stones are left in the cherries). In Limousin, *milliard* is called *clafoutis*. *Madeleines* are spongey cakes. Marzipan is made in St Léonard.

CHEESES

Cheese is used in many dishes, including chicken (see recipe). But Auvergne cheeses are superb in their own right. Cantal (*fourme de Cantal* or *fourme de Salers*) is one of France's greatest cheeses. Nutty, not unlike Cheddar, it is made in factories all the year, but farm cheese made June to September is far better. It comes from around Aurillac. Cantal is one of Europe's biggest volcanic craters.

Tomme d'Aligot is nutty but slightly sour. Tomme de Brach is a sheep's cheese with pronounced smell and flavour. Bleu d'Auvergne is a firm sharpish blue cheese made mostly in factories. Bleu de Causses and bleu de Thiézac, made on farms, are superb between June and November. Bleu de Laqueuille, scarce, matured in caves, is almost Roquefort standard, though made of cow's milk. Fourme d'Ambert has rich blue marbling and very strong flavour. Only farms of Forez mountains still make it. Murol (flat disc with pink rind with a hole in the middle) is supple and mild. Creusois (or Guéret) is made from skimmed milk and is low fat. So is strong gaperon, flavoured with garlic. Made on farms, it used to hang in pear-shapes from farmhouse beams and many were a sign of wealth (now it is dome-shaped).

One of the best cheeses, especially when farm made, is St Nectaire, matured on rye mats in damp cellars, rich, slightly tangy – made from very fresh milk. Three farm-made goats' milk cheeses are cabecou d'Entraygues (creamy, firm), chevrotin du Bourbonnais (supple, creamy, truncated cone, mildly nutty), and rigotte de Pelussin (May-November, firm, nutty).

WINES

The main wines of Auvergne, Saint-Pourçain and Côtes d'Auvergne are classified as 'vins de la Loire' but are nothing like Loire wines. Whites are closer to cheaper white Burgundy, reds like a rustic Beaujolais, and they go very well with regional food. Whites of St Pourçain made from Chardonnay and Sauvignon grapes with a local Tresallier are dry, fruity and have finesse.

Seek wines of the co-op or of Maurice Faure. Reds, made from Gamay or Pinot Noir or both, are light, sappy and easy to drink but not so good as the whites. Côtes d'Auvergne red wines have improved greatly. Chanturges and Chateaugay, made like Beaujolais from the Gamay grape, are well worth seeking. Drink young and cold. Very pale rosé of Corent is popular locally. Whites can be acidic. Further south, dry whites and light reds from Marcillac, Entraygues and Estaing are all right for everyday quaffing. But drink all these wines young (1 to 3 years old).

16

LANGUEDOC/ ROUSSILLON

Though Languedoc is France's biggest wine-producing area, little is used in cooking. And although most cooking is peasant and fairly solid, herbs and spices are used liberally. Montpellier was for centuries a spice port and Arabs influenced cooking, too. In the south and east, olive oil, tomatoes and aubergines dominate many dishes while pork and goose fat, mushrooms, chestnuts and dried beans are used a lot in the north and west, with garlic popular everywhere. On the coast you will notice inevitably a Provence influence. Here fish often have confusing Catalan or even Basque names. Hake, for instance, called *colin* elsewhere, becomes *merluza* or *merluche*. We solve the problem by picking out one which looks nice and pointing to it! Whereas in the mountains and around Toulouse and Albi most fish comes from the Basque Atlantic port of St Jean de Luz, known especially for its Atlantic tunny (*thon*), the south gets shellfish from Thau lagoon outside Sète (oysters, mussels and clams called

Chestnuts

palourdes) cultivated on loosely woven nets. They are in season June to September and usually eaten raw with vinegar and chopped shallots or grilled on a *brochette*. You can sometimes buy them ready-stuffed with sausagemeat *à la Sétoise* to be braised in olive oil with shallot, tomatoes and, of course garlic. Sète is an important fishing port and supplies fish of many types, notably sardines, anchovies (*anchoïs* or *anchoïo*), Mediterranean tunny (more delicate and a fifth of the size of Atlantic *thon* and often called *thounina*), *rascasse* (scorpion fish – essential ingredient of Provençal *bouillabaisse*), and a fish with spikey head which we did not even know in English – gurnard (*grondin*). *Langouste à la Sétoise* is a spiky lobster sautéd in oil and served with a piquant sauce of tomatoes, brandy, garlic and shallots, suspiciously like *Armoricaine* or *Americaine* sauce.

The staple diet of peasants and even fishermen until recent times was *Brandade du morue* (creamed salt cod with lots of garlic) (see recipe).

Fresh anchovies, fried, are made into a paste called *anchoïade*, with garlic and oil, eaten spread on toast, as a dip for raw vegetables, or with fresh figs. You can buy it ready-made.

A simple soup is *aigo bouido* (garlic soup with oil and egg, poured over bread slices) (see recipe). There are many fish soups, some similar to *bouillabaisse* but with more solid white fish, no *rascasse*, and sometimes with potatoes, such as *aigo saou*. You can make up your own version.

The mountains supply excellent sausages, often air dried, and hams. Look for sausages labelled *fabrication montagnarde* or something similar. Try raw mountain ham the local way, with fresh figs or superb local radishes, for breakfast, or as a starter or light lunch. Better still, serve it in spring with young, raw broad beans (*fèves*). The French take the outer layer off broad beans, making them sweeter and more tender. Sausages are often fried in goose-fat and served with thick spiced tomato sauce.

Genuine Toulouse sausage is superb, but there are some lesser factory versions, so buy it at a charcuterie or boucherie. The meat and fat should be hand-cut in largish lumps, and some grains of pepper should be included. It needs to be cooked. Usually it is sautéed in pork fat with garlic and herbs and served with tomato, parsley and capers. *Boudins* (black puddings) of Béziers contain pine kernels. *Galabart* is a large black pudding, *melsat* is a white sausage (*boudin blanc*) of pork, not chicken. The *marinoun* is a giant air-dried pork sausage rather similar to *rose de Lyon*.

Chickens, turkeys and ducks abound in this area, though most ducks are intended for *foie gras*. Fields are stubbly for sheep rather than lush for cattle. Though they are proud of their lamb and mutton, the meat is often tough, proved by the number of recipes in which it is stewed or braised, including *ragoût* with the inevitable white beans, and *épaule de mouton à la catalane en pistache* (shoulder of mutton *en pistache*) (see recipe). Then there are sweet mutton minced pies (*pâté de Pézenas*) which you can buy at a charcuterie or pâtisserie and are eaten as a snack, savoury or dessert. They are made of brown sugar, minced mutton, mutton fat, beef suet and grated lemon peel in pastry and are delicious.

With the tomato and aubergine, golden fleshed pumpkins (*citrouilles*) are the standbys of Languedoc. They are used not only for sweet cakes and tarts but as vegetables, in bread and in soup (see recipe).

Languedoc looks north as well as south; winters are rigorous and some popular dishes are too heavy for midsummer heat near the coast. That is true of *cassoulet*, the fortifying dish of white beans cooked with different ingredients in Castelnaudry, Carcassonne and Toulouse versions. All have a base of beans, pork rind, garlic, onion, cloves, bay, thyme and parsley. Carcassonne adds lamb or mutton, Toulouse adds lamb or mutton, Toulouse sausage, and *confit* of goose or duck. No true *cassoulet* lover would tolerate such additions as tomatoes, used in Montauban.

Cassoulet-making is a religion, so never state a preference. Only make it if you have time to devote entirely to it. But you can keep it simmering for days or heat it up so that you can help yourself when you are hungry.

You can buy it in tins and pots but beware of cheap supermarket versions. We have given a Toulouse recipe. You must soak the beans for some hours to make them sweet but not ferment. You should use goose fat (*graisse d'oie*) which you can buy in tins and you must sprinkle the dish with breadcrumbs, stir in the crust that forms, then sprinkle more crumbs. Do this seven times!

A local delicacy is pig's liver, salted, dried, pressed and smoked (*foie de porc salé*). It is rolled like a sausage. Slice it, fry quickly in olive oil, then serve as a salad (*fêche sec*) with sliced radishes, quartered hard-boiled eggs and artichoke hearts, sprinkled with wine vinegar and oil.

Crème d'Homère (wine and honey cream) is a delightful sweet, easy to make – a richer *crème caramel* (see recipe).

Languedoc has excellent early fruit. Red cherries of Céret are perfect for cherry tarts. Kiwi fruit is grown, too.

CHEESES

We have included Roquefort elsewhere though it is technically of Languedoc. Bleu de Loudes cow's milk cheese from farms has a fine strong flavour but little smell (also called bleu de Velay). A lovely soft farm goat's cheese, with a nutty flavour, is pélardon des Cévennes (also called d'Anduze). Rogeret des Cévennes is similar. Passe l'an from Montauban is a large hard cow's milk cheese cured for 2 years, low-fat and used much like Parmesan of Italy. Various cabecou cheeses of goat's milk were named after 'cabre', a word for little goat in the old Langue d'Oc (local language).

WINES

Languedoc-Roussillon has been called Europe's wine lake because it still produces about 40 per cent of French wine, despite attempts to change to new crops, such as rice. For long much of the wine was rubbish, produced for blending to make cheapest *ordinaire*. Replanting with different grape varieties and general improvements mean that many better *vins du pays* are being produced.

Some very drinkable reds are produced, especially deep-red Minervois, which ages well. Corbières wines from hills south-east of Carcassonne are solid and fruity. Best are Fitou and Côtes du Roussillon. Costières du Gard wines are fruity, refreshing and cheap.

White wines are inferior, though La Clape is fresh and fruity. Muscat sweet wines of Frontignan and Rivesaltes are pleasant as an aperitif as well as for dessert and Banyuls Grand Cru, aged in wood for at least 2½ years, is a really excellent sweet wine.

Blanquette de Limoux sparkling white is deservedly becoming popular all over France, though produced since the sixteenth century.

17

BORDEAUX, GASCONY, LES LANDES

Bordeaux is a gastronomic centre where the Bordelais have developed regional dishes to complement the variety and finesse of their wines. This is the only area of south-west France where butter is used for cooking.

Food is very often chosen to fit the wine, which is why beef is the most popular meat in an area devoted mostly to the goose and pig. Gironde's Bazas beef is best for *entrecôte Bordelaise*, they say. Lambs grazed on salt marshes of the Gironde (*agneau de Pauillac*) are as succulent as Charentes and Normandy's *pré-salé* lamb, but appear from January to April. Later lamb comes from Gascony where the saddle is cooked with garlic (*Gasconnade*). In Les Landes lambs are fed with milk. In the pine forests geese and duck are made into *confit* you can buy in cans and jars. Delicious chicken fed on maize come from St Sever in Les Landes.

Bordeaux gets superb vegetables and fruit from surrounding districts such as Lot et Garonne and in the city's big, fine market, held every day except Sunday, you can see little mountains of them for sale – green beans, big knobbly tomatoes and fine asparagus from Marmande, artichokes and little potatoes from Les Landes, tiny white radishes for salads, yellow haricot beans, small carrots with plumes of feathery leaves, red cabbage, shallots used as freely here as garlic is further south. There are two types of aubergine – Toulouse (white inside) (see recipe) and Barbetane (green flesh). Les Landes potatoes are sautéed in goose fat with onions and chopped cured ham.

Fruit includes black Chasselas and white Muscat grapes (*raisins*), red skinned fleshy plums (*prunes*) dried to make *pruneau d'Agen* (tart) (see recipe), outdoor strawberries (*fraises*), mainly in May but still around in June and delicious served in red wine, nectarines (June to September), peach (*pêche*) from June to September, greengages (*reines-Claude* – July, August) and Kiwi fruit (November to April) originally from Yangtse River, developed in New Zealand, grown here as an alternative crop to ordinary wines and beloved by Nouvelle chefs for décor.

Fifty varieties of edible fungi grow in Les Landes forests, including some truffles (*truffes*) and more *cèpes*, the fleshy brown autumn mushroom with no peer (see recipe).

Bordeaux gets eels and shellfish from the Gironde estuary and the Arcachon basin, where oysters, *palourdes*, cockles, and mussels are kept in concrete pens. Oysters are sold in sizes 0 to 6, with 6 as the biggest. A disease struck the oysters in 1970 (some say it was really an enthusiast using weedkiller in the pens) and native varieties died off. They were replaced by Pacific gigas, fast growing, large and more rubbery, so often cooked.

The custom is to serve oysters with *pâté de campagne*, *grattons de Lamont* (pork potted in its own fat) or preferably small peppery sausages, such as *crépinettes*, grilled and hot. You swallow an oyster, eat a bite of bread and butter, take a mouthful of sausage, then a good draught of dry white wine – no lemon juice or vinegar with the oysters, which must be cool, not iced. James Bond would have known.

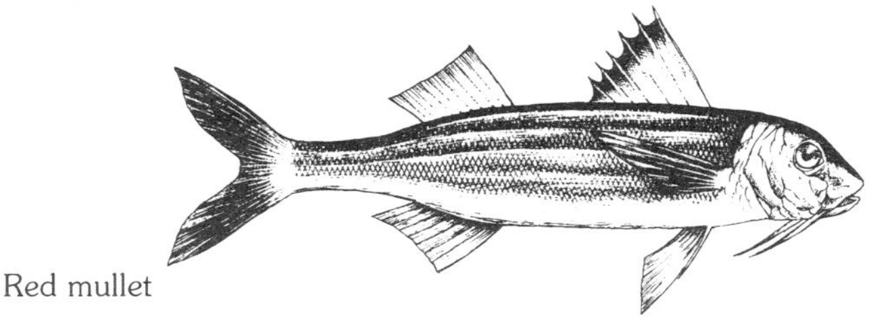

Red mullet

The Gironde boats bring in excellent red mullet (*rougets*) (see recipe) and lampreys (*lamproies*). These are eel-like fish which are stewed with leeks, mushrooms, onions, chopped

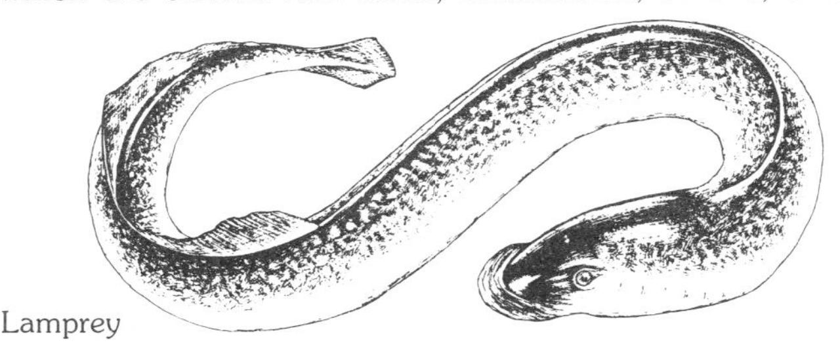

Lamprey

ham and red wine. They can be bought ready-cooked in cans but are expensive. If you cook them yourself, remember to take out the poisonous cord running down the lamprey's back. It could kill you. Henry I, who died of a surfeit of lampreys, was probably killed this way.

St Emilion, famous for cakes and pastries, produces macaroons (*macaron*) which are delicious with fruit in red wine (raspberries, strawberries, peaches). *Pastis* in Gascony is a pastry made of folds of paper-thin pastry moistened with Armagnac or Cognac and baked with butter and sugar. In Bordeaux shops it is called *gâteau Landais*. With a layer of prunes or apples, it is a *croustade*. *Pruneaux fourrés* are very expensive but you can buy a single one. They are prunes stuffed with prune *purée* and almond paste. Marzipan (*massepain*) is sold shaped like sardines or shellfish.

CHEESE

Few good cheeses are produced here. The Bordelais used to eat Dutch Edam with their wine – a hangover from the days of big trade exchanges with Holland. Poustagnacq, a fresh sheep's milk cheese of Les Landes, is best in winter.

WINES

Bordeaux wines are remarkable not only for quality but variety. The British think that the French drink them too young, which is why some Frenchmen prefer Burgundy.

The five top areas are: Médoc (probably the best wines in the world); St Emilion (two bad years for the merlot grape have forced up prices); Pomerol (all red); Graves (best white and very good red); Sauternes/Barsac (all sweet white).

Top Médoc wines are divided into 5 *crus* (growths), all very expensive. Sauternes has Grand, Premier and Deuxième *crus*. Graves offers a list of top classified wines. St Emilion has Premier Grand Cru and Grand Cru wine (confusing), then Appellation Contrôlée. For a digestible run-down of classes and vineyards, take with you David Peppercorn's *Pocket Guide to the Wines of Bordeaux* (Mitchell Beazley).

Bordeaux has an enormous choice of Appellation Contrôlée, Bourgeois Supérieur and Bourgeois wines which are more affordable, extremely drinkable and often underrated. Fronsac and Côtes de Canon Fronsac produce charming wines still developing for 6 years. Côtes de Blaye and de Bourg, on the 'wrong' side of the river from Médoc, make simple, highly-drinkable reds which can be drunk when 3 years old (the French drink them one year old!). Bourg wines are heavier (try de Barbe and du Bousquet). They also produce dry white wines.

Lalande de Pomerol reds are much underrated and can be drunk younger than Pomerol (try Moncets, Anneraux, and the fruity Siaurac). Lesser St Emilions (Montagne, Lussac and Puisseguin) can sometimes be better than AC St Emilions (try Belair-Montaiguillon, Laurets, Maison Blanche when young, and especially Château St Georges). Entre-Deux-Mers produces a lot of highly drinkable dry white wine (try Launay and Moulin de Launay). A good red from here comes from André Lurton at Château Bonnet. Among many good Cru Grand Bourgeois Médocs (excellent value) are La Cardonne, Cissac, Fourcas-Dupré, Du Glana (St Julien), Les Ormes-de-Pez and especially Phelan-Ségur (St Estèphe). Look particularly for the words 'Grand Cru Bourgeois Exceptionnel' (there are only 18).

Armagnac is at the base of Gascony, near the Pyrénées. Many Frenchmen prefer Armagnac brandy to Cognac. It is distilled only once and is earthier. It becomes much dearer with age but not necessarily better. The best is from Lower (Bas) Armagnac, that of Upper (Haut) Armagnac is often used for pricey bottles of fruit in brandy. Floc de Gasconne (a good aperitif) is made of grape juice and Armagnac – like Pineau de Charentes.

18

PAYS BASQUE, BÉARN & THE PYRÉNÉES

Basques are neither French nor Spanish (unlike Catalans who are a blend of both) and though they borrow from both countries their cuisine, like their culture, is individual. Béarn, inland, the High Pyrénées and Ariège are basically French in their cooking with an inevitable mountain background of butter, game and pork. Most of that splendid cured Bayonne ham comes from Béarnais pork, cured in salt in Bayonne. Though we eat it cut very thin and raw, locally it is cooked in many dishes. Look for other mountain hams – cheaper than Bayonne, sometimes chewier.

Both Basques and Béarnais use a lot of beans and cabbage, pork and goose. Goose fat, which you can buy in pots, is used in Béarn for cooking meat, frying eggs and even for cooking trout. Try it – most interesting. Incidentally *sauce Béarnaise* was invented in Paris.

Béarn hillsides support vast flocks of sheep for Pyrénéan wool, milk for making cheese (much of which is sent to Rouergue to make Roquefort) and for lamb and mutton. The mutton here is sweet and delicious – well worth trying. Buy a shoulder or leg cut off the bone, and stuff it with chopped garlic, shallots and parsley, mixed with breadcrumbs soaked in wine and bound with beaten egg. You lay out the meat, smear it with stuffing, roll, tie up and cook in a brisk oven. Deglaze the pan with wine, shake in it slices of red and green peppers, deseeded and blanched and serve them and the winey juice with the meat.

In Béarn too are produced many of the sweet peppers (green and red) which are the mark of Basque cooking. Beware – they are called *piments Basquais* here, not *poivrons*, as in most of France, where *piments* can mean chillies and *piment Basquais* can mean paprika! The Basques like hot flavours, however. Try the small Bayonne spicy garlicky sausages *lou kinka*. As in Bordeaux, these are served hot with oysters. Local black pudding called *tripotchka* is made with veal or mutton and is spicy. You can sometimes buy it cooked or you must simmer it for 2 to 3 hours in *bouillon* with onions, carrot and herbs. Tarragon is popular. It is said to be an aphrodisiac. Marjoram (*majolaine*) is used freely and parsley in vast quantities.

As in Périgord, you can buy *confit* of goose in cans or jars, but it is usually called *lou trebuc*. It is often added to the great dish of Béarn which has spread north through Gascony and right through the Pyrénées and Basque country – garbure, a superbly sustaining soup-stew of varying ingredients – cabbage, garlic and haricot beans (always), broad beans, other vegetables, herbs, ham and preserved pork, turkey or goose, served separately while the soup is poured over a slice of bread (see recipe). You must leave a little soup, add wine swill it round and drink it (called 'chabrot' here, 'chabrol' in Gascony).

Bayonne is the sophisticated centre for cooking and shopping for food. The excellent market is on Tuesday, Thursday and Saturday mornings. Even fried eggs are spectacular in Bayonne (*oeufs frites à la Bayonnaise*). You fry as many eggs as you can eat in olive oil and stack them on bread fried in olive oil with a slice of fried Bayonne ham between each. *Pipérade* is a delightful dish with eggs (see recipe). Smoked meats – ham, chicken, turkey, pork are in charcuteries.

The joy of eating in the Basque country is the fish – salmon from the River Adour, cooked in a red-wine *court-bouillon*, superb wild trout from Pyrénéan streams, and a multitude of fresh fishes landed at St Jean de Luz, one of Europe's biggest fishing ports, which supplies fish to towns and villages of the Pyrénées as far as Albi and Toulouse. Apart from popular fish like sole, hake and sea bass, St Jean specialises in cuttlefish (*chapiron*), angler (*baudroie*), gurnard (*grondin*), octopus (*pieuvre*), grey mullet (*mulet*), squid (the Basque name is *chipirons*, often served stuffed

Cuttlefish

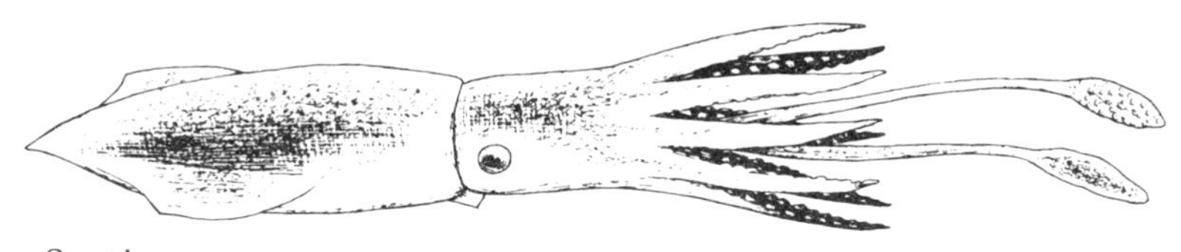

Squid

and stewed with tomatoes in their own ink), and excellent *langoustines*. Above all, in season superb Atlantic tunny fish (*thon*) is landed.

St Jean de Luz and the fishing harbour across the river at Ciboure are the best places to try *Ttoro*, also called *Thoro*, the Basque fish soup. Very similar to *bouillabaisse* of Provence (see recipe).

In the mountains, a little wood pigeon (*palombe*) is very tender. Marinade, then braise it in white wine and brandy. Serve with puréed artichokes.

Chocolate was first made in France by Jewish refugees from Portugal in Bayonne, which is still famous for it. Basques love cakes, as you will see in the pâtisseries. *Gâteau Basque* is a custard pie usually with rum. Pumpkin bread (pumpkin, corn with rum) is eaten like cake. Marzipan is sold in many shapes. *Ttouron* is an almond nougat vividly patterned with hazelnuts, pistachios and crystallized fruit. In summer Pays Basque produces fine figs, plums, cherries and dessert grapes.

CHEESES

Orrys from Ariège is one of the best of many mountain cheeses (cow's milk, pressed, uncooked, spiced, peppered and strong, often grated onto food). Ossau and Iraty are matured creamy cheeses with an earthy flavour, made from milk of two types of sheep. Bethmale (cow's milk from Ariège) has a strange but pleasant sharp taste. Esbareich, made of sheep's milk in mountain cottages, is mild when young, strong after 4 to 6 months.

WINE

Do try Madiran red wine if you can get it. Made of a local grape, *tannat*, mixed with *cabernet*, it is deep purple, with high tannin when young, developing richness later. Jurançon moelleux (sweet) white wine is rated second only to Sauternes by many and is delicious with strawberries. It is strong (16 to 18 per cent). Look for Cru Lamouroux. Jurançon dry white, not so highly rated as the sweet, is flowery and full, with a taste of honey and nuts. Very drinkable young, both wines go a lovely amber colour with age and have a slight taste of nutmeg. Try Clos de la Vierge.

Irouléguy, from a mere 100 acres of vines around St Etienne de Baïgorry near the Spanish border, produces a very pleasant red from *tannat* grapes, also lesser white, and rosé. Inevitably shops carry a lot of Spanish Rioja. The red has greatly improved in the last 15 years, but prices have risen.

Izarra is a herbal liqueur made in Bayonne from herbs of the Pyrenees; like Chartreuse, in strong yellow version, very strong green. The monks of Chartreuse were banished to the Spanish side for some years. Izarra is served as an aperitif on ice (*frappé*), as a liqueur, and used in cooking desserts.

19

PROVENCE, SOUTHERN RHÔNE & CÔTE D'AZUR

The sun, sea, olives and wild herbs make Provençal cuisine – thyme, oregano, savory, rosemary, fennel, wild lavender. Olive oil is used for frying, flavouring, enriching; garlic for enhancing taste. Provence without them would be like Bordeaux without wine. Garlic laces the mayonnaise called *aïoli* (see recipe) served with poached salt cod (*morue*) or cooked and raw vegetables – artichokes, beetroot, salsify, asparagus, chick peas, green beans cooked or raw, raw carrot, celery and cauliflower. Vegetables are superb, from the tender sweet young broad beans, wild and cultivated asparagus and violet (small globe) artichokes of early spring to cauliflowers and the second crop of artichokes and many mushrooms in autumn. Swiss chard (*blette*) and spinach (*épinard*) are popular and are made into a sweetish tart with sugar, raisins and cream (see recipe).

There are superb tomatoes from April to November, of

Fennel

course – plum and big knobbly 'beef' tomatoes. See them piled high in the markets, from the permanent covered markets of Marseilles and Nice to the delightful weekly market on Tuesdays in the streets of Vaison-la-Romaine in the Vaucluse. Stalls are ablaze, too, with Charentais and Cantaloup melons, apricots (*abricots*), cherries (*cerises*), peaches (*pêches*) from June to September, pears (*poires*) and red-fleshed plums (*prunes*) from July to September, nectarines mid-July to mid-August, and table grapes (*raisins*) August to October. Much fruit is imported from Italy and North Africa, too. You are most likely to find the home-grown local varieties in Vaucluse, north-east from Avignon, and the Bouches-du-Rhône. Beautiful strawberries (*fraises*) are produced here from March to May. Steep them in red wine – delicious! You can get old French *reine de reinette* apples (*pommes*) as well as the almost-tasteless Golden Delicious, which are neither golden nor delicious.

Young broad beans are around in March and early April. They are splendid eaten raw, dusted with salt, as a starter, with olives and sliced sausage. Later, when bigger, the outer coating is peeled off before lightly boiling or steaming. That makes them greener and more tender.

This is a splendid area for vegetarians or anyone cutting down on red meat. *Ratatouille*, the summer vegetable stew, eaten hot or cold, as a starter or as a vegetable dish with meat, is made of whatever vegetables are abundant – aubergines, tomatoes, red and green peppers; courgettes are the most popular, gently stewed in pure olive oil with no water, always with garlic and some onions, usually with herbs, especially basil. You can deep-freeze it, but if you keep it in

Basil

an ordinary fridge, boil it up each day to stop it fermenting. *Tomates Provençales* are tomatoes topped with olive oil and garlic and grilled.

You can buy stuffed vegetables in shops but we would not buy them from a market stall or scruffier shop; nor would we buy *petits gris* (local snails) stuffed with herb-butter at similar places. For a light beach lunch, buy or make *pan bagna* (bread moistened with olive oil, spread with chopped tomatoes, sweet peppers, anchovies, onions and olives). *Salade Niçoise* is made of segments (*not* slices) of tomatoes, radishes, green and red peppers, broad beans or French beans, onion, perhaps artichoke hearts or tunny fish with anchovies, hard boiled eggs and black olives, lettuce (optional), dressed with olive oil.

Try to buy olive oil from an oil mill. The best is 'vierge extra'. 'Vierge fine' is slightly more acid, 'semi-fine' or simply 'vierge' still more acid. The quality really matters with most Provençal dishes. The local joke is that 'fish is a creature found alive in water and dead in oil'.

Mediterranean fish is difficult for foreigners because there are types which are never seen in their waters, like *rascasse* (scorpion fish), an essential part of *bouillabaisse* with conger eel (*congre*) and gurnard. There is no authentic *bouillabaisse*. It was started by fishermen on their boats. They had a pot with olive oil in it and threw in one of each fish they caught – 'one for the pot'. You must include garlic, onions, tomato, herbs. It is similar to *thoro* but it must include saffron and not hake. All sorts of fish are added – monkfish (*lotte*), gurnard (*grondin*), red mullet (*rouget*), whiting (*merlan*). In Toulon they include potatoes, to the fury of the Marseillais. Never waste expensive shellfish like lobster in it – long boiling destroys the taste.

Although charcuteries in this whole area of Provence and the Rhône offer a wide choice of sausages, most are imported from other areas. The great exception is *saucisson d'Arles* (Arles sausage) which used to hang from rafters of country kitchens to dry. You serve it in a starter-dish of charcuterie, as a snack with bread and olives to accompany wine or to add flavour and perfume to stews. Arles sausage is three-quarters pork and one-quarter beef from cattle of the Camargue, with black peppercorns, paprika and garlic, and in our view is the best of its kind in France, especially if you can buy it from a farmer or small butcher who has hung it to ripen in a drier (*séchoir*). From some charcuteries or boucheries you can buy *caillettes* – meatballs of chopped pork liver with blanched chard or spinach.

Local beef is not very good, which is why it is so often larded with pieces of pork fat, marinaded in wine, then simmered for 3 hours or more very slowly in wine with bacon, herbs and vegetables. This dish — the *daube* — is still a part of autumn, winter and early spring life in the country (see recipe). Most beef is imported now, but still cooked this way. Mountain lambs of Sisteron area and lowland lambs of Arles both feed on wild herbs as well as grass and have a distinctive flavour loved by locals and gourmets. But they are not so tender as the *pré-salé* lambs of the north and those which are not spit-roasted when very young are still given the tenderising *daube* treatment. This takes time — marinading overnight and cooking for 4 or 5 hours just below boiling point — but is very rewarding. Provençal cooks deliberately make too much, put the leftovers in the fridge overnight and serve it cold next day in its own jelly. Octopus gets the same treatment.

Desserts are simple — superb fresh fruit, dates (*dattes*), roasted chestnuts (*marrons*), fresh figs (*figues*) dried figs with

Figs

walnuts, raisins and peeled almonds, quince jelly (*gelée* or *pâté de coing*, from pâtisseries), nougats or *la pompe* (orange or lemon flavoured bread-cake which you dip in wine — sometimes called *lou gibassie*). Aix-en-Provence makes delicate, expensive almond biscuits with crystallised fruits called *calissons*. In the Nice area pâtisseries and boulangeries sell whole, or slices of, *la socca* (chickpea pancake) which you eat in the street with salt or sugar.

CHEESES

Favourite is brousse, fresh unsalted sheep's cheese, mild,

white, creamy, farm-made, often served with fruit. Banon, commercial version of brousse, is wrapped in chestnut leaves except when mixed with summer savory (called *poivre d'ai* or *pèbre d'âne* – donkey's pepper). It can be made with sheep's, goat's or cow's milk. Sarriette is very creamy commercial cheese. Tomme de Camargue, Arlésienne or Gardien is sheep's milk cheese flavoured with thyme.

WINE

King of southern Rhône red wines is full-bodied, richly scented Châteauneuf-du-Pape, most of which is ready for drinking after 4 years but can be kept longer. Heavier wines last longer ('78's are superb but avoid 1975). Château Rayas is magnificent but rare. Domaine de Mont Redon is easiest to find and very good. Beaucastel and Chante Cigale last well. Beaurenard is one of the new lighter wines. Some cheaper Châteauneuf, especially those bottled elsewhere, are not so good. Clos des Papes red and white are good. White is fairly rare but worth seeking. Gigondas produces a deep-coloured red which starts almost mauve and ages excellently – at its best after 6 to 8 years. Once much under-estimated, it is becoming fairly expensive. Do try it, especially Domaine St Gayan and Château de Montmirail. The co-operative wines are good, so are those of Roger and Gabriel Meffre and Pierre Amadieu.

Côtes du Rhône Villages wines are better and stronger than the ordinary plain Côtes du Rhône wines. Try Vacqueyras red (fruity and heavy), Roaix (good value), Séguret, Sablet and Laudun. Tricastin and Côtes de Ventoux reds are improving noticeably and are good value. Lubéron makes very drinkable red, white and rosé. So does Lirac, where wines have improved fast. Rosé of Tavel is generally regarded as the best rosé in France. A heavyish wine – don't ice it. Serve cold with food.

Muscat de Beaumes de Venise is a delicious sweet wine, served chilled as an aperitif or dessert wine. Drink it young for real flavour.

Provence is known to tourists for its dry, strong, perfumed rosé, pleasant cold with fish. But Bandol wines, particularly red, have improved greatly and are underestimated – smooth, strong, all kept 18 months in wooden casks. They age well. Try Moulin des Costes and Mas de la Rouvière of the Bunan family and Domaine Tempier. Bandol's only real rival in red wines in Provence is the strong pricey Château Vignelaure – a Coteaux d'Aix-en-Provence wine. Reds and whites of Côtes de Provence are improving but many of the best are overpriced. Good wines include Château Minuty from Gassin, Domaine de St Maur at Cogolin, also Château Ste Roseline, and Château de Selle (rather pricey). As Hugh Johnson said: 'Most Provence wines get by on a lot of alcohol and a pretty colour.' Try the unusual Château Simone from Palette, a tiny appellation (if you can get it).

The best white of Provence is Cassis, heavy with an interesting taste, much drunk with fish soups.

20

FRANCHE-COMTÉ (JURA), SAVOIE DAUPHINÉ

These three mountain districts on the Swiss border have a completely different history but much in common in farming and food. All produce superb mountain cheeses, freshwater fish and all rely heavily on pork. Traditional dishes are hearty and designed to keep out cold. Though fashionable ski resorts and big towns have turned to 'international' food, smaller towns and villages still live on traditional dishes and provide the fine fresh ingredients.

All districts have great traditions in curing meat and producing superb charcuterie (called *cochonailles*). Smoked mountain hams are superb (try *Luxeuil*). In Franche-Comté look for *Jésus de Morteau*, dried salami-type sausage, and *brési*, beef dried over wood fires and thinly sliced. Both are eaten raw or put in *potée* (stew). *Saucisses au cumin* (Montbozen sausage) includes *anis*, a plant flavouring Pernod, which is made at Pontarlier on the Doubs river. Herby sausages from Annecy (*pormonniers*) are served cooked (see recipe). Game comes from wild forests of Jura foothills (try Besançon game pâté). From lowlands of Franche-Comté come excellent vegetables and fruit, especially cherries.

Apart from trout, pike and perch, the Savoie produces from lakes Annecy and Geneva (called Léman in France) rare members of the salmon family – *lavaret, omble chevalier* and *féra*. They are usually served in cream sauces flavoured with rarer fungi – *morilles* or *cèpes. Lotte des lacs* and *Lotte de la rivière* are different types of *burbot* (firm fleshed pike-perch).

Rare and dear but truly delicious are the white truffles of Savoie. You can buy them in cans, but if you do get a fresh one, put it in a covered bowl with eggs in their shells for two days then make omelette or scrambled egg (with cream) and add chopped truffle. The truffle aroma, stronger than in black truffles, infuses the eggs. In late summer a lesser known vegetable is cardon (*cardoon*), a coarser celery usually braised or baked with cheese. *Courge* (vegetable marrow) is made into soups with cream or served *au gratin*.

Cardoon

Gratin dishes are legion in Savoie and Dauphiné, especially with cheese on top. But an authentic *gratin Dauphinois* should not have cheese. We have that on the authority of the Dauphiné Tourist Board in Grenoble, who got so tired of cheap imitations passing themselves off as this great dish that they have printed the true recipe in their tourist brochure. We have given this recipe – without cheese. But we put cheese on half the dish – for Arthur, not Barbara. It makes a good supper, or vegetable with plain grilled meat, and leftovers are excellent cold.

Gratin Savoyard is thinly sliced potatoes baked in meat stock with cheese covering. Gratins are made of leeks (*poireaux*), pumpkins, Swiss chard (like spinach), mushrooms, minced meat, ravioli and crayfish tails (*queues d'écrevisses*), usually with cheese on the top, but sometimes breadcrumbs or both.

In charcuteries of Dauphiné try *murcon* (sausage with cumin – caraway seed), *sabodet* (boiling sausage), *caillettes* (faggots made of minced pork liver and pork with herbs – delicious), *diots* (Savoy vegetable and pork sausage, preserved in oil – cook it in wine). Cakes and pastries are many. Pognes is a *brioche* crown with fruit in the centre or pumpkin in autumn. *Biscuit de Savoie* is light sponge cake with almonds. *Gâteau Grenoblois* is rich walnut cake (Grenoble walnuts are so good that the French government have given them an Appellation Contrôlée and they appear in many desserts and sweets). *Mont Blanc* is meringue with chestnut *purée* and whipped cream. Pâtisseries offer many fruit 'tartes'. *Foyosses* are *brioches* with varying elaborate fillings. Almonds from Drôme are used for macaroons and marzipan cakes. Chambéry produces superb liqueur-flavoured chocolate truffles, served sometimes instead of dessert. *Pets de nonne* of Jura are little fritters of *choux* pastry (literally 'Nun's farts').

CHEESES

Cheeses are superb and used as the basis of cooking everywhere. French gruyère is richer and tangier than Swiss. The two types are Comté and Beaufort, made in Savoie mountain farms. *Fondue* is a dish of these three mountain districts as much as of Switzerland (see recipe); not to be confused with *fondu*, a smaller, creamier gruyère. Morbier is coarser, fruitier. Cancoillotte is a yellow, fruity, runny cheese sold in cartons and eaten warm on toast. It includes butter, garlic and eggs. Chevret is a soft, nutty goat's milk cheese made on farms in Jura (best June to November).

In Savoie and Dauphiné there are many cheeses called *tome* or *tomme*, all cow's milk except, of course, tome de chèvre from goats of Haute Savoie, tomme de Vercors (goat's) and tommes des Allues from Miribel eaten in autumn. Tome de fenouil is fennel-flavoured. Tome aux raisins is ripened in a dry mixture of grape skins, pips and stalks which flavour it. Tome de Sixt is kept several years until hard and tough, so often grated for *au gratin*. Tomme means 'cheese' in local Savoie dialect and Tomme de Savoie is made by farms, dairies and factories – cow's milk, softish, low fat.

St Marcellin, once made on farms from goat's milk, is now factory made from cow's milk but a few farms make a delicious goat's milk version called tomme de St Marcellin. Beaumont and Trappiste de Tamié (made by monks) are softish mild creamy cow's milk cheeses similar to St Paulin.

Reblochon, known since the fourteenth century, is the great cheese of Haute Savoie, semi-hard with delicate flavour, weighing around 500g and sold in a wooden box. Dairymen in old times did not milk the cows dry, then made a second milking for their own benefit when the steward had gone. The cheese they made was the *rebloche* (perk).

Very good blue cheeses include bleu de Sassenage, softish cow's milk, made for centuries in Dauphiné (best June to November), persillé des Aravis, goat's milk from Savoie (summer and autumn), bleu de Tignes, cow's milk (summer and autumn).

Brochette Jurassienne is square pieces of cheese wrapped in raw mountain ham stuck on a skewer and fried in butter.

WINES

Vin jaune of Jura is sherry-like, through long ageing in the cask. As with Fino sherries, a mould (*flor* in Spanish, *le voile* here) is allowed to grow on the wine. It tastes to us like Montilla, is expensive, but makes a super *Coq au Vin*. Château-Chalon is best. Vin de paille is a gold, sweet wine made from grapes dried on small mats. Red, white and rosé table wines are light and drunk young. Vin gris is not grey but rosé! Production is dominated by Henri Maire of Arbois (very reliable). As in Switzerland and Alsace, Franche-Comté produces many highly alcoholic fruit brandies, such as Kirsch, distilled from cherries, and Mirabelle from plums.

Savoie wines are white, red or rosé. Whites are mostly dry, light, very refreshing. Seyssel is good and rare, it is also made sparkling. Crépy is often *pétillant* (tingling on the palate). Frangy from Roussette is very drinkable. Reds are light in weight and colour. Try Bugey.

Chambéry makes a superb white vermouth from wine and mountain herbs. From the Carthusian Monastery near Grenoble comes the delicious herbal liqueur with a big kick – Chartreuse. It is traditionally yellow (strong) or green (stronger) and is still used to relieve colic in people and, as a 140 per cent elixir, in cows. A strawberry version is now made for tourists.

21

ALSACE & LORRAINE

Twice occupied by Germany, set at a true junction of Europe, and now saddled with EEC offices and staff at Strasbourg, Alsace and its neighbour Lorraine have inevitably absorbed the cooking of many areas. But there is always something different about their versions of dishes. And one of those differences is their lavish use of their own Riesling wine.

Not even a German city offers a wider range of charcuterie and sausages (such a help to self-caterers who want to eat like local people yet have time to see and enjoy all they can). And no other area of France has such a diversity of breads, pies and cakes, with spices, dried fruits or pork fillings, *brioches*, *kougelhopfs*, fruit tarts and savoury flans such as *quiche Lorraine*.

You will find such a feast of tempting ready-cooked and ready-baked delicacies in the shops that if the weather is fine you will not want to bother much with cooking. Pastry rules. Even *pâté de foie gras*, that expensive, controversial and (let's face it) delicious pâté of the liver of force-fed geese, is cooked in pastry (*en croûte*). Beside it on the charcuterie board may be any of 40 types of sausage, including some to be cooked, such as *saucisse de Strasbourg*, a bigger, thicker Frankfurter served grilled and sliced or in hotpots (it can be bought in cans) and *boudin à la langue* (black pudding with lumps of tongue, poached inevitably in Riesling). Big *tourtes* (pies), usually of chopped veal and pork, are sold by the slice, and medium-sized *tourtes* either in slices or whole for bigger or hungrier families (see recipe). Look out for *porcelet en gelée* (pork in aspic), pork liver *terrines*, smoked fillet and loins of pork and different smoked bacons and hams. Ham of Colmar is poached. Tasty, light *bouchées à la reine* (big *vol-au-vents* filled with chicken or ham in cream sauce) are sold ready to heat in the oven.

Fruit tarts are made not only of fresh fruits in season (including excellent red and white currants and greengages), but dried apples, plums, pears and apricots (*schnitz*) which are also cooked and served with game and meats. Even local supermarkets have a splendid choice of jams, fruit conserves for eating with the interesting local breads, filling tarts or eating with cold meat, and fruits in *eau-de-vie* to give you a dessert and a drink. Apple slices are often fried in pork fat to serve with sausages. And there are very tempting chocolate-covered fruits. Do try *birewecke* (fruit bread) made with dried pears, apples, figs, plums, raisins, white almonds, walnuts, flavoured with cinnamon and Alsace Kirsch (black cherry spirit). *Kougelhopf* is tasty, too – a sweet light *brioche* ring with raisins, currants and almonds, soaked in Kirsch. *Quetsches* (purple plums) are made into spirit of that name and into tasty pie (*tarte aux quetsches*) (see recipe).

You can buy plenty of vegetables from other areas but, locally, cabbage rules – green, white, red and sauerkraut (*choucroute*), pickled white cabbage cooked in pork or goose fat with beer or Riesling. You can buy it tinned, but if you can get it from the barrel at least it *seems* better. It is served with game, beef but especially with pork and sausages. A real Alsatian *choucroute garnie* is very filling and much nicer than you might think (see recipe).

Cucumbers are grown under cover from February until October and, like long white radishes, deep red beetroot, potatoes and wild fungi such as *morilles*, are served with a cream sauce as salad. Cold dishes with salad are very popular. *Gelée de canard*, for instance, is a delightful starter, or light meal with salad, excellent for slimmers and lovers of 'modern' cooking though it is an old dish of Strasbourg. You might be able to buy it ready-made (see recipe). Asparagus is excellent in April and May. It is served with poultry as a vegetable or cold in salads or hot with ham. Young dandelion greens (*pissenlits*) are included in spring salads.

Trout are plentiful, and are used with pike, perch and eel to make a *matelote* (fish stew) cooked in Riesling. Do try cooking *sandre* in Riesling (see recipe). A cross between pike and perch, it has a delicate flavour. It is usually served with noodles – a popular and useful accompaniment to fish or meat. Alsacien Riesling does give a more fragrant flavour to dishes than most white wine. *Coq au Riesling* tastes totally different from chicken in red wine.

Game of Alsace and Lorraine, particularly the Vosges, is excellent fresh in season or canned in pâtés, *confit* or prepared dishes out of season, when fresh wild rabbit (*lapin de garenne*) takes over. Pâtés can be bought *en croûte* (baked in pastry). *Marcassin* (young boar) is little different from pork, but *sanglier* (boar) makes excellent bacon. Venison (*cerf* and *chevreuil*) is often jugged (*étouffade de cerf*). Pheasant, partridge and hare are fairly plentiful. Game is most often made into a *civet* – stewed very slowly with bacon, onion and herbs in wine in which it has been marinaded. Dry white wines are used in Alsace and Lorraine and are drunk with game, too.

Lorraine's famous *potée* is made very like that of the Auvergne (see recipe). It includes bacon rind, fresh fatty pork (belly), knuckle of ham and a large pricked sausage.

Baba and *baba à rhum* (rum baba) come from this area and are always in the shops. *Bretzel* (pretzel biscuits in knot shape) are eaten sweet with tea or coffee, savoury with wine. Other confectionaries you can buy are *bredles* or *petits four à l'Alsacienne* (rich buttery biscuits), *bergamotes* (square sweets made of honey), *crêpes Alsaciennes* or *pfannekusche* (thick pancakes topped with fresh or preserved fruit and much cream), *kaffeekrantz* (iced cakes eaten with coffee), *lebkueche* (gingerbread biscuits, often heart-shaped), *tarte à la Linz* or *linzertorte* (sweet tart of pastry with almonds and Kirsch, filled with soft fruit conserves, such as raspberry or redcurrant, covered with latticework pastry, it makes an excellent dessert) and *madeleines* (shell-shaped cakes of Nancy). *Tartes* to look for include rhubarb, bilberry, whortleberry, wild cherry (*merise*) and blueberry. Some pâtisseries sell vacherin – a glorious confection of crystallized fruit, ice cream, whipped cream and meringue.

CHEESES

Munster cheese from the Vosges mountains of Alsace and Lorraine has its own Appellation Contrôlée, no less! Soft, supple, tangy with a powerful smell, it is glorious when made in farms or local dairies (summer and autumn), still good made in factories (Munster *laitier* – all year). Mild when young, it becomes rich and spicy later. Nothing to do with Ireland – the name comes from the Latin *monastorium* (monastery). Farms also make it flavoured with caraway seed (*cumin*), the spice cumin, or anis. Other cheeses: St Rémy (strong, spicy, factory cow's milk cheese from Lorraine); Bibbeleskas (*fromage blanc* – fresh cheese, used in cheesecakes and tarts or eaten mixed with horseradish and herbs); trappiste d'Oelenberg (smooth round mild cheese made by Trappist monks at Oelenberg Abbey); géromé (supple, ripe cow's milk cheese with strong smell, often flavoured with fennel or anis – not to be confused with géromé des Vosges which is mild cured Luxeuil ham).

WINES

Alsace wines are dry, refreshing, fruity, attractive and basically should be drunk young except wines marked *reservé*. These are wines from good years which should be kept five years. They are named after their wine types and growers have concentrated on perfecting Riesling in recent years, at the expense of Sylvaner. Sylvaner wines are fresh and fruity but lighter. Riesling is very dry, with a delicate smell and taste. Gewurtztraminer is fairly dry but heavier, spicier and loved usually by people who don't drink much wine. Good for elevenses or with desserts. Muscat d'Alsace is really fruity and still dry. Worth trying. Tokay d'Alsace (grape called pinot gris elsewhere) is dry (unlike the great Hungarian Tokay), full-bodied and earthy rather than fruity. Pinot Blanc wines are being developed and improved. Pinot Noir one of the Champagne grapes, is usually made here into a fruity rosé with a fine bouquet.

Edelzwicker is a name of blended wines, usually with a lot of Chasselas grapes. Very good wine producers are Hugel, Trimbach, Dopff and Irion, Dopff au Moulin. A lot of 1983 Rieslings and Tokay were good enough to keep five years; 1984 wines are for drinking now. It is almost too late!

Alsace and Lorraine both produce many fruit spirits. Lorraine produces *ratafias* of fresh fruit juice mixed with spirit made from the fruit. *Ratafia de noyau* is made from kernels of peaches and apricots. It tastes of almonds.

22

CORSICA

Like the Corsicans themselves, flavours of their cooking are strong and aggressive and simple traditional dishes reflect hard times in Corsican history. This is not criticism. Fewer convenience foods are sold here than almost anywhere in France and if you can avoid too many imports, it is a pleasure to feed off simple, strong-tasting dishes rather than simple bland dishes fashionable elsewhere.

Fish is still superb. True, *langoustes* (spiny lobsters without claws), once cheap here, are now rushed to Paris. Corsicans eat sea-urchins (*oursins*) instead – either boiled or washed, raw. Be sure to open them by cutting with scissors on the concave side and draining off liquid and rubbish. Cockles and winkles are popular, too. But best are sardines (fried in batter or grilled) and red mullet (grilled and served with black olives). If you stay near fishermen you might get a delicious delicate fish called *mostelle.* Cook it immediately – it deteriorates fast – cleaned, oiled, dusted with flour, very gently grilled. Trout from the mountain rivers is superb. Just grill in oil with a light touch of fennel or thyme. Fish stew (*ziminu*) is much like Basque *Thoro*, spicier than *bouillabaisse.* You can put almost any white fish or shellfish you like in it, but must serve it with *pebronata*, a sauce of red peppers, tomatoes and garlic stewed in oil, like the Italian *peperonata* but spicier and including juniper berries (see recipe). This is served with meats and game, too.

Corsica was several times under Italian rule of one sort or another and the influence on cooking and local language is obvious. *Stuffatu* (like Italian *stufato*) is the same dish of beef marinaded and stewed in red wine with peppers, tomatoes, garlic, onions, a little bacon and herbs. Try to get locally-produced meats – lamb, beef, pork, even mutton and goat. These will almost certainly be tough, so marinade them overnight, preferably in wine, if not, in oil, aromatic vegetables and herbs, then braise in wine. The flavour is delightful, for they take on a little of the flavour of the thick maquis which strays to their pastures — juniper, thyme, myrtle and heathery arbutus. Pigs feed on the windfall chestnuts, too. You are most likely to find this meat in village boucheries or markets inland, especially in the mountains. The taste is more obvious in the game — woodcock, partridge, pigeon, and wild boar. The season begins in the autumn, but game is conserved in cans and bottles, and made into excellent pâtés you can buy all the year (make sure that you get the local pâtés, though). Boar is made into good rough mountain ham, still sold in the villages. *Prisuttu* (seasoned and smoked cured ham) is delicious. In the

Prisuttu

charcuteries you will find, too, *copa* or *coppa*, highly-spiced shoulder of pork served sliced, highly-spiced sausages with the same name *copa*, *figatelli* (spicy sausages of pork and liver sold raw or cooked), Lonzo (fillet of pork dried and salted, eaten raw in wafer-thin slices as *hors d'oeuvre*), and *sangue* (blood pudding).

Under Italian rule, Corsicans had to pay taxes by exporting their wheat, so chestnut flour took its place. Though rarer now, with a European grain mountain, it is still used to make many delightful breads and pastries. *Polenta* (or *pulenta*) is like Italian *polenta* but made with chestnut flour, not maize. The flour is quite sweet. *Polenta di Castagna* is a chestnut flour *purée* (see recipe), served hot with *sangue* or *figatellis*, both of which you poach, or with poultry, game and meatier fish. *Polenta de Châtaignes* is a chestnut flour cake or biscuit served like bread, or fried in oil or topped with ham or preserved pork as a sort of sandwich. It can be made with cheese and butter in it or not (see recipe). *Brilluli* is chestnut flour porridge, served with milk or cream. *Panizze* is a chestnut flour cake. *Castagnacci* is a chestnut flour flan. *Fritelles* are chestnut flour fritters seasoned with fennel and served with cheese.

The favourite delicacy of Corsicans is *merle*, made into pâté or baked inside a rasher of fat bacon. We have not tried it. It is blackbird, a protected species in Britain. A good snack, from shops or on bread from snack bars or take-aways, is *anchoïade*, anchovies puréed into a paste with garlic, herbs and olive oil (sometimes onion or even with figs), used as a dip for raw vegetables or spread on bread and put under the grill, sometimes topped with cheese.

Plums, peaches, cherries, almonds abound, and olives, of course, but the most succulent fruits are Corsican figs.

CHEESES

Herds of sheep and goats in the foothills provide many local cheeses. Much of the sheep's cheese is now sent to Roquefort to be matured in those famous caves, but you can buy bleu de Corse. The major cheese is broccio (or brocciu), cheese of goat's or occasionally sheep's milk, often with a sharp taste. It is used in *falulella*, a cheese-cake and *fiadone* (cheese and orange flan) which you can buy in shops. Broccio is nice cooked in omelettes flavoured with mint or used in a salad of tomato, cucumber chunks, red and green pepper slices and onion, dressed in olive oil and dusted with herbs (like a Greek salad). Broccio is used to stuff sardines before grilling them and is grated over pasta. A soft, herb-flavoured cheese (goat's or sheep's) is called brindamour. Imbrucciate is a local cheese tart you can buy in shops.

WINE

Like so many French wines once drunk or blended as *ordinaires* or ignored by 'serious' winesmen, Corsican wine has improved greatly. There is strong Italian influence in the grape types. Patrimonio, a strongish red for drinking with meat and game, is made mostly from the Nielluccio grape, a relation of Sangiovese used in making Chianti (try Clos de Bernadi and Clos Marfisi). A rosé is made here, too. Other good areas are Coteaux d'Ajaccio, Sartène, Porto-Vecchio (try Fior de Lecchi) and Figari (try Poggio d'Oro). Cap Corse produces an interesting dry white wine Clos Nicrosi and a very interesting heavy, sweet raisiny white Muscatellu, a Muscat Doux Naturel, reminiscent of *vins doux wines* of Frontignan if not in the same world as Beaumes-de-Venise.

Cap Corse, a wine-based aperitif using local herbs, is one of those drinks which seem more attractive drunk cold under the noonday sun than when you get home.

For long, Corsican wines were grown only on precipitous hillsides. Since malaria was banished from the plains vast new plantings have been made in the last 30 years. All Appellation wines are called 'Vin de Corse', but most of the production is still very ordinary *Vin de Pays*, much of it being shipped in bulk to strengthen weak table wine elsewhere – or, alas, to the wine lake.

23

RECIPES

Recipes have been put under the names of the regions where they originated or became most popular, but you will often find very similar dishes in other regions of France.

Each recipe is basically for four people unless otherwise stated, but appetites are hard to judge, especially in modern days of diets and weight consciousness.

Imperial equivalents can be found in the Weights and Measures section at the end of the book.

SAUCES AND DRESSINGS

Picardy and the North

Chou Rouge Flamand (red cabbage)

1 red cabbage
3 large (tart) cooking apples
1 teaspoon brown sugar
pepper
vinegar
butter
salt

Cut a red cabbage into quarters, wash and shred, cutting out hard core and stem. Season with salt, pepper and sprinkle with a little vinegar (preferably cider). Put into a casserole with butter (no water). Put on lid. Cook on gentle heat. When cabbage is three-quarters cooked, add cooking apples, peeled and cut into thick slices, and brown sugar. Finish cooking on low heat. Probable total cooking time 2 hours.

Endives à la Flamande (chicory in butter)

500g chicory
1/5 litre water
salt
2 tablespoons butter
1/4 lemon (juice)

Put chicory into a saucepan with butter, juice of quarter lemon, pinch of salt, and the water. Cover, bring to boil, simmer slowly for 45 minutes. Put chicory in vegetable dish, stir more butter into cooking stock and pour over vegetable. Do not cut the chicory before cooking; it will taste bitter.

Brittany

Beurre Blanc (butter sauce)

100g unsalted butter
3 shallots
few drops lemon juice
6 tablespoons dry white wine (or 3 tablespoons wine, 3 tablespoons wine vinegar)

Served usually with pike or shad — *brochet* or *alose* — but also with any fish likely to be dry.

Chop shallots finely, boil them in small saucepan in the wine until reduced to 2 tablespoons of liquid. Take off heat. Cut butter into little knobs, whisk two knobs into liquid until creamy, put on very low heat and whisk in the butter knob by knob. Season. Add lemon juice.

Paris and Île de France

Sauce Béarnaise

3 tablespoons wine vinegar
2 tablespoons white wine
1 shallot, finely chopped
*1 tablespoon chopped parsley (*persil*)*
*1 tablespoon chopped tarragon (*estragon*)*
*sprig of thyme (*thym*)*
fragment of bay leaf
4 tablespoons butter
3 egg yolks
salt

Usually served with steaks or fish.

Boil shallot with half the parsley and tarragon, salt, thyme, bay, in wine and vinegar, reducing by a third. Take pan off heat, strain, cool a little and stir in egg yolks. Transfer to top of double-boiler or *bain-marie*(any bowl over a saucepan of very hot water). Melt butter and whisk into sauce slowly.

When smooth and thick as mayonnaise, pour into sauceboat and add rest of parsley and tarragon.

Sauce Bercy

2 shallots, finely chopped
125ml white wine
600ml brown or beef stock
2 teaspoons arrowroot mixed with equal water
1 tablespoon parsley

For meat, usually steak.

Boil shallots in wine until reduced to 1 tablespoon. Add 3/4 of the stock. Whisk arrowroot paste into boiling stock gradually until it is like very thin cream. Season to taste. Fry steaks in oil, transfer to hot plate. Reheat sauce. Add reserved 1/4 stock to frying pan juices and boil, stirring well. Strain into the sauce. Add chopped parsley.

Périgord, Quercy and Rouergue

Farce aux Marrons

150g raisins
1/2kg tinned whole chestnuts (or 1kg if using for garnish)
liver of bird or a few chicken livers
3 tablespoons butter
thyme
salt
pepper

A simple chestnut stuffing for turkey or any poultry or game.

Soak raisins for up to 12 hours; drain chestnuts; chop liver. Cook liver in heated butter for 2 minutes. Remove from pan; add 2 tablespoons butter to pan, add chestnuts, thyme, salt and pepper; cook over medium heat for 5 minutes, stirring. Leave to cool. Mix chestnuts, drained raisins and liver together and put inside bird. Roast bird. As garnish, cook another 1/2kg of chestnuts in butter with salt, pepper and a teaspoon of thyme.

Massif Central

Chou Rouge à la Limousine (red cabbage with chestnuts)

1 red (medium) cabbage
4 tablespoons pork fat (French lard)
20 peeled (or tinned) chestnuts
bouillon

As served with pork in Limousin, but pleasant with any roast – takes 2 hours.

Shred and moisten cabbage with a little stock or *bouillon*; add pork fat and 20 peeled or tinned chestnuts, chopped. Season, cook very slowly with lid on for about 2 hours.

Provence, Southern Rhône and Côte d'Azur

Aïoli (Garlic Mayonnaise)

6 cloves (large) garlic
2 egg yolks
lemon (juice)
½ litre olive oil
salt
pepper

For serving with salt cod, soaked, then boiled, lightly-cooked vegetables, hard-boiled eggs or raw vegetables-crudités.

Crush garlic, add egg yolks, a little lemon juice, salt and pepper, then work in olive oil gradually, as for mayonnaise.

Corsica

Pebronata (sauce or side vegetable)

1 kg red peppers
1 kg ripe tomatoes
1 large onion sliced
2 sliced garlic cloves
6 juniper berries
pinch of thyme
4 to 5 tablespoons olive oil
peppers
salt

Herbs to taste; when serving with lamb, rosemary is an obvious choice.

Deseed peppers, cut into strips; skin tomatoes, chop roughly. Cook onion and garlic in olive oil until golden. Add peppers, cover pan, cook gently for 15 minutes. Add tomatoes and salt. Cook for further 30 to 40 minutes until tomatoes are in a thick sauce and peppers are quite soft. Liquid should all be absorbed by peppers, so if dish is still too runny towards the end, take the lid off for last few minutes.

Polenta or Pulenta

*225g chestnut flour (*farine de châtaigne*)*
1 litre water
2 tablespoons salt
Optional – 60g butter
75g grated cheese

Serve as purée side dish to meat, poultry or fish or hardened into 'bread' as suggested in recipe.

Bring water and salt to rapid boil. Sprinkle in chestnut flour very slowly, stirring all the time with a wooden spoon. When mixture is thick and smooth, cover pan and lower the heat. Cook for 30 to 40 minutes (until mixture comes away from sides of pan). Now serve very hot as a purée, or stir in butter and cheese and serve as a light meal. With or without cheese, it can be cooled spread on a flat wet surface to go hard. Cut into squares, cover with tomato, pebronata or other sauce, bake in a moderate oven or fry in oil and butter until golden and serve sprinkled with cheese. Or coat in egg and breadcrumbs and fry in deep oil like fritters.

SOUPS

Picardy and the North

Soupe à la Bière (beer soup)

2 teaspoons fine sugar
1½ litres light beer
salt
pepper
⅕ litre cream (thick)
butter
flour
cinnamon
2 eggs

Make ½ cup of light roux with butter and flour, pour onto it, gradually over a very low heat, the light beer (preferably already warmed). Mix until smooth. Add salt, pepper, pinch of cinnamon and fine sugar. Bring to boil, simmer for 30 minutes. Mix thick cream with two eggs and pour into liquid to thicken just before serving.

Paris and Île de France

Potage aux Primeurs (spring vegetable soup)

leaves of 2 celery heads
half a cos lettuce
white of 3 leeks all cut in thin strips
3 spring onions, sliced thin
150g uncooked green peas
2 litres beef or chicken stock (we prefer chicken)
6 egg yolks
salt
pepper

Invented by Carème, chef to the Prince Regent and later to

Csar Alexander I.

Simmer vegetables with salt and pepper in stock until tender (10 to 15 minutes). Whisk egg yolks in a bowl. Stir in 4 tablespoons of hot soup and whisk this into main soup. Serve with croutons (5 slices firm white bread, decrusted and diced, fried in 60g butter and 60ml oil).

Soupe à l'Oignon Gratinée (onion soup)

250g onions, sliced finely
1 tablespoon butter
25g flour
2 litres beef stock or consommé
sliced French bread
dash of brandy (optional)
150 to 175g Gruyère cheese
salt
pepper

Fry onions in butter until soft but not coloured; sprinkle with flour, stirring. Add stock, salt, pepper and simmer for 30 minutes. Toast the bread or crisp it in oven. Put soup in ovenproof casserole (preferably earthenware), sprinkle each bread slice with grated cheese, float them on the soup, sprinkle more cheese over the top and heat in hot oven until cheese is brown.

Languedoc/Rousillon

Aigo Bouïdo (garlic soup)

4 egg yolks
4 tablespoons olive oil
8 cloves garlic
4 tablespoons cream (optional)
lightly toasted sliced bread
bay leaf
thyme
1 litre water
salt
pepper

Make a mayonnaise with oil and egg yolks. Boil water with garlic, sprig of thyme, bay leaf, salt and pepper. When garlic is well cooked, crush into a paste. Remove thyme and bay, put back paste into water. Put mayonnaise in tureen, pour garlic water over it, add cream, stir. Serve ladled over toast.

Soupe à la Citrouille (pumpkin soup)

1½kg pumpkin
250g dried white beans
2 onions, finely sliced
2 (medium) potatoes
meaty knuckle of bacon
100g pork fat
3 cloves garlic
½ litre milk

bouquet garni	*1½ litres water*

Soak beans overnight. Peel pumpkin, cut into large pieces. Peel and slice potatoes. Simmer beans, bacon, onions and *bouquet garni* for 60 minutes in water. Add pumpkin, potatoes, pork fat (very finely chopped), garlic, season, simmer for another 60 minutes. Take out knuckle, remove bacon meat, cut in small pieces, put back in soup. Add milk. Serve poured on dried bread slices.

Bordeaux, Gascony and Les Landes

Soupe des Vendanges (grape-pickers' soup)

Made in harvest time in enormous pots, possibly an old laundry boiler. Quantities of each item don't matter so long as beef is plentiful. Slits are made in a large piece of beef and into them are put spices, garlic, salt, pepper, bay and seeds of fresh grapes. The beef is put in a big pot with a piece of leg of veal and whatever space is left is crammed with leeks, garlic, turnips, cabbage, celery, rosemary and a bunch of mixed herbs, salt and plenty of pepper. Fresh grapes and plenty of cloves are added. All is covered in water and boiled hard until the liquid is reduced to one third. Then it is simmered for hours until the meat is cooked, the juice is *bouillon*, which is served separately as soup. You have meals there for several days.

Pays Basque, Béarn and the Pyrénées

Ttoro (fish soup-stew)

2 carrots	*2 sprigs parsley*
2 onions (large)	*fish heads*
3 cloves garlic	*olive oil*
1½ litres water	*bay leaf*
½ litre white wine	*flour*
thyme	*pepper*
2 tomatoes (or paste)	*red peppers*
cayenne pepper	*red chilli*
1 (large) leek	

Don't bother with expensive shellfish — it looks pretty but loses much taste with long boiling. Exact quantities of fish do not matter. The Basques use mostly conger eel (*congre*), gurnard (*grondin*), angler fish (*baudroie*), hake (*merluz*), and scorpion fish (*rascasse*), plus mussels and scampi and fish heads.

Fry fish heads in olive oil, add the water and wine, carrots and onions; crush 2 garlic cloves and chop the white part of the leek. Add to the mixture with parsley sprigs, thyme, bay leaf, tomato paste or two tomatoes. Boil and reduce for 2 hours to make stock. Strain. Clean and scale fish, cut into chunks and put in a pan. Sprinkle with flour, tomato paste, pepper, cayenne pepper, and another chopped clove of garlic. Wash mussels and add to fish. Stir and add strained stock. Add seeded red peppers cut in strips and one small seeded red chilli, finely chopped. Bring to the boil, add scampi, simmer for 5 minutes. Pour over slices of bread rubbed with garlic.

STARTERS

Picardy and the North

Flamiche (leek tart)

leeks
butter
egg yolks
cream (optional)

Cook white sliced leeks slowly in butter. Line a buttered tart tin with ordinary pastry. Blend leeks with yolks of eggs and cream (if using), season. Put this in tart case, cover with a thin layer of pastry. Press edges together and crimp. Bake in very hot oven.

Brittany

Galette

buckwheat flour
fried egg
sausage
bacon
chopped ham

Prepared in the same way as crêpes but use buckwheat flour (*blé noir*), no sugar or cream. Fill with fried egg, sausage, bacon, chopped ham or anything savoury, then roll. Bretons sometimes fill them with anchovy paste.

Loire and Western Loire

Pâté de saumon et Mousse de Cresson (salmon pâté with watercress mousse)

¼ litre (almost) milk
75g butter
100g flour
2 small eggs
350g skinned fish
½ tablespoon fresh cream
½kg salmon
For mousse: 150ml stiff mayonnaise
150ml whipped cream
bunch watercress
pinch paprika

The white fish can be pike, whiting or plaice. It must be skinned and boned — as must be the salmon.

Make a smooth sauce with heated milk, 60g butter and 60g of the flour. Bring to boil and cook for a few minutes, stirring. Remove from heat, add lightly beaten eggs, one at a time. Mince white fish very finely and add to mixture with the cream, remaining butter and seasoning. Line a terrine dish with the fish mixture and arrange salmon in the centre. Cover with rest of mixture. Cook for about 1¼ hours in a covered *bain-marie* (180°C, 350°F, Mark 4). Leave to cool. Make the mousse by mixing all ingredients in a bowl with seasoning. Serve with the pâté.

Périgord, Quercy and Rouergue

Mousse de Roquefort aux Noix (Roquefort mousse with walnuts)

100g Roquefort cheese
100g butter
100g fresh cream
50g shelled walnuts

Served as a starter or savoury with toast or a spoon.

Whip the cream. Liquidise cheese and butter, fold carefully into whipped cream. Fold in the walnuts and serve.

Omelette Périgourdine (omelette with truffles)

8 eggs
1 tablespoon goose fat (or pork)
truffle about egg-size or 2 smaller, chopped in cubes
salt
pepper

Housewives put eggs in their shells with truffles in a bag for several hours to impart flavour to eggs. A traditional recipe included small cubes of goose liver as well as truffles.

Beat eggs with salt and pepper. Add chopped truffles (and goose liver if used) and make either one large or two smaller omelettes. Pour the juices from canned truffle onto it before serving. Gourmets eat it with Sauce Périgueux, but this takes so much effort to make properly that we do not think you will want to spend the time on holiday, even if you spend the money on two or three more truffles.

Truffe en Chausson (truffle 'turnover')

Medium to large truffle
100g foie gras *(preferably goose; if not, duck)*
2 thin slices smoked streaky bacon
For pastry: 250g flour
150g butter
salt
beaten egg for glazing

Make shortcrust pastry, put in fridge for 2 hours, roll out into an even circle. Chop liver. Lay bacon in middle of pastry, spread with chopped liver; put truffle on top, wrap bacon round it; brush edges of pastry with water, fold it over like a turnover. Double fold edges and crimp them with large fork. Brush with beaten egg, place on buttered baking pan. Bake 20 minutes (at 220°C, 425°F, Mark 7). Cover top lightly with foil if in danger of burning.

Massif Central (Limousin, Auvergne, Bourbonnais)

Bleu d'Auvergne Soufflé (cheese soufflé)

100g bleu d'Auvergne cheese mashed
2 eggs, separated
25g flour
25g butter
¼ litre milk
grated nutmeg (optional)

For starters, savoury or light supper.

Make a roux by melting butter and stirring in flour until smooth. Add milk gradually, stirring constantly, season and add pinch of nutmeg. Cook for about 10 minutes. Add egg yolks one at a time. Stir in cheese. Whisk egg whites until stiff and gently fold into mixture. Butter 20cm soufflé dish or several small *ramekins*. Fill with mixture only two-thirds full. Bake uncovered for 20 minutes (at 180°C, 350°F, Mark 4), then raise for 10 minutes (to 220°C, 425°F, Mark 7).

Pâté Creusois (potato and pork pâté)

Use same ingredients as in Pâte de Pommes de Terre (below) but add 250g fresh belly pork, seasoned with a little dry white wine, replace shallot with clove of garlic. Line a 30cm diameter circular baking pan with half the pastry. Season potatoes with salt, pepper, garlic, parsley. Chop pork. Fill lined pan with a layer of potato and cream, then the pork. Cover with other half of pastry, glaze with egg. Put in hot oven at first, then lower. Cook for 60 minutes.

Pâte de Pommes de Terre (potato and cream in flaky pastry)

500g flour
250g butter
400g potatoes
1 chopped shallot (or ½ onion)
1 beaten egg
*100ml fresh cream (*crème fraîche *or single cream)*
pinch of chopped parsley

For pastry: rub fat into flour and salt. Make a well in middle and add enough water to make a fairly stiff dough. Leave to rest for 30 minutes, preferably in fridge. Cut into halves, roll out into two circles. On one spread potatoes cut very thin, seasoned, shallots and parsley. Leave border about 2cm round edge, wet border with a little water. Cover with second circle, roll over the two borders to seal. Glaze with egg. Cook in hot oven (200°C, 400°F, Mark 6) for 1¼ hours. When pâte is cooked, cut tiny circle in top and pour in the cream. Serve hot as starter, supper or with main course.

Bordeaux, Gascony and Les Landes

Aubergines Landaise

5 to 6 aubergines
350g raw smoked gammon in strips
100ml olive oil
75g tomato purée
3 cloves garlic crushed
salt
pepper

Slice aubergines lengthwise, sprinkle with salt and leave to sweat for 2 hours or so. Drain and wipe dry, cut into thick slices and cook gently in oil to soften. Add gammon, stir for about 10 minutes (gammon should begin to colour). Add tomato purée, garlic, pepper and more salt if needed. Stir well, close cover; cook over slow heat for 30 to 40 minutes.

Cèpes à la Bordelaise

1 kg cèpes
3 cloves garlic, crushed
2 large shallots chopped
1 wineglass olive oil
2 tablespoons chopped parsley
salt
pepper

Other wild mushrooms can be used but not button mushrooms.

Remove mushroom stalks, chop stalks very finely, mixed with parsley and garlic. Cook mushroom heads gently in oil with salt and pepper without letting them get too soft. Add the chopped mixture, cook for another 5 minutes. Eat at once on baked croûtons or to accompany meat.

Pays Basque, Béarn and Pyrénées

Pipérade (peppers, tomatoes, and onions)

6 good-sized tomatoes
2 large onions
2 large green peppers
2 large red peppers (or 1 red and 1 small hot red chilli)
2 cloves garlic
6 to 8 eggs
3 tablespoons olive oil
1 teaspoon chopped parsley (optional)
salt

With eggs, usually served with lightly fried Bayonne ham as a starter or light meal.

Chop peeled onions and garlic, soften in olive oil over moderate heat. Add deseeded and chopped peppers, chilli (*very* finely chopped). Peel, quarter, deseed tomatoes and add. Cook gently until vegetables are soft and juice has nearly gone (15 to 20 minutes). Beat eggs with salt and parsley, add them, stir until they are cooked but not dry.

Franche-Comté (Jura), Savoie and Dauphiné

Fondue Savoyarde (Savoy fondue)

500g each of French Emmental, Comté and Beaufort cheeses or 1,500g of any one
1 clove garlic
1 litre dry white wine
pepper
*1 tablespoon cornflour (*fécule de maïs*)*
150ml Kirsch (spirit distilled from black wild cherries)
1 loaf of French bread

You do really need a table burner or hot plate for this dish.

Derind cheeses and cut in thin slices. Rub the inside of a saucepan with peeled garlic. Boil wine in saucepan and add cheese. Stir until cheese melts. Add pepper. Dissolve cornflour in Kirsch, pour into saucepan and stir until smooth and slightly thickened. Cut bread into cubes. Serve immediately on a spirit or candle burner or hotplate to keep mixture from hardening. Each person dips bread cubes on a fork and scoops up the fondue. If you have no burner, it can be served spread on toast, but is not so much fun. We have seen Frenchmen eat it on *frîtes* (chips)!

FISH

Normandy

Sole à la Dieppoise

Cleaned sole (or turbot, plaice or John Dory)
1 onion or three shallots finely chopped
1/4 litre very dry cider (or Muscadet wine)
butter
1/2 litre thick cream
mussels
shrimps

This is a recipe from the Dieppe Cookery School; cook fish whole; allow about 300-400g per person.

Butter fireproof dish generously, sprinkle shallot, put in fish seasoned with salt and pepper. Pour over cider. Cover with buttered paper, put in oven (190°C, 375°F, Mark 5), basting every 5 minutes, for 15 minutes. Remove buttered paper, stir in 300ml of the cream, put back paper and cook for 15 minutes more. Poach some mussels and shrimps in cider or wine for garnish. Remove fish to hot dish, pour sauce into saucepan, add rest of cream and knob of butter, heat on ring until reduced to a smooth, thick velvety sauce. Pour over fish, garnish.

Sole au cidre

Cleaned sole, left whole (or turbot)
3 chopped shallots
2 tablespoons chopped parsley
very dry cider to cover fish (1/4-1/2 litre)
butter
salt
pepper

For dieters avoiding cream.

Put sole in buttered oven dish, surround with shallots and most of parsley, sprinkle with salt and pepper. Add cider. Cook in preheated oven (160°C, 325°F, Mark 3) for 25 to 30 minutes. Sprinkle rest of parsley over fish before serving.

Brittany

Burbot en Ragoût de Moules (burbot in mussel stew)

1,000g filleted burbot
800g mussels
½ litre fresh cream
200g onions
200g leeks
300g sliced potatoes
⅓ litre Muscadet
50g butter
bunch of chives

Other white fish could be used, especially *lotte* – monkfish.

Cook mussels in Muscadet. Slice leeks, onions, potatoes. Fry burbot fillets, then onions and leeks in butter. Add the mussel liquor. Remove burbot fillets and keep hot. Add potatoes and cream. Season. Cook for 15 minutes and reduce. Add the shelled mussels. Cover fish fillets with the sauce and sprinkle with chives, finely chopped.

Mouclade (mussels in cream sauce)

3 litres mussels
1 medium onion
bouquet garni *of parsley, bay leaf, sprig of thyme*
¼ litre Muscadet
300ml cream
knob of butter
chopped parsley

The mussels to be scrubbed scraped and washed; the onion finely chopped. In a large saucepan, soften onion in butter. Add herbs and mussels. Pepper lightly, add wine. Cover, shake over fierce heat for a few moments until mussels open and cook. Transfer mussels only to a large heated dish. Remove any mussels which did not open. Keep hot in low oven. Remove *bouquet garni* from liquid, quickly stir in cream and pour over mussels. Serve with lots of bread to mop up cream sauce. (In Vendée, a little curry powder is added.)

Loire and Western Loire

Mousse Chaude de Brochet au Coulis d'Ecrevisses (hot pike mousse with crayfish purée)

600g boned pike
4 egg whites
1 litre cream
For purée: 1kg crayfish (or prawns)
1 litre fish stock made with pike bones and head
100ml Cognac
100ml cream
1 tablespoon butter
1 tablespoon flour

Salmon trout can be used as an alternative to pike, which we prefer, and prawns for crayfish, which we don't.

Pound fish or put through electric blender with salt and pepper. Add egg whites. Mix well. Stir in cream. Butter a mould (preferably ring mould), fill with mousse, put in *bain-marie* and cook for 45 minutes in oven (180°C, 350°F, Mark 4).

To make purée: scald crayfish or prawns if uncooked (take out little black intestine); peel crayfish tails or prawns; crush shells and fry in butter; add Cognac; reduce by half; add fish stock, cook for a few minutes over low heat. Strain. Season. Thicken a little with flour and butter. Add cream. Unmould mousse, arrange crayfish tails in centre or round it, pour sauce over it.

Poitou-Charentes

Bar Poché (poached sea bass)

Sea bass clean and scaled (usually about 2½ to 3kg)
25 black peppercorns
bottle of dry white wine
court-bouillon
salt

Can be served hot or cold.

Season inside of fish with salt and wrap tightly in cheese cloth or muslin because bass is delicate and liable to break up. Put it in a fish kettle or large saucepan (if saucepan is too small, do not curl fish into it. Cut fish in half or in large segments). Add peppercorns, some salt, the wine and enough *court-bouillon* to cover the fish.

Put saucepan on high heat. When scum forms, lower to 'simmer'. Simmer for 25 minutes if fish is to be eaten hot, 15 minutes if you are eating all of it cold. For hot dish, drain, unwrap, serve with *beurre blanc* or lemon juice. To serve the whole fish cold, leave it to cool in the stock.

Bouilleture d'Anguilles (stewed eels)

1 kg eels
1 bottle of red wine (Champigny)
1 glass of marc (spirit)
2 tablespoons butter
1 tablespoon flour
thyme, parsley, bay leaf
For garnish: 200g small onions
200g little mushrooms
6 slices bread, all fried in butter

This recipe will serve between 4 and 6 people.

Our advice: buy the eels (preferably small Poitevin eels) ready skinned and cleaned. Wash, cut into sections, put into stewing pot and cover with red wine. Season, add herbs. Bring to boil, add glass of marc, flambé. Cook for 15 minutes. Remove pieces of eel. Thicken cooking liquor with tablespoon of butter and of flour, stirring in well. Strain sauce over the eels. Serve with garnish (above).

Moules au Pineau des Charentes (mussels in Pineau)

Mussels (cleaned — allow ½ litre per person)
shallots (4 to 6 each)
1 tablespoon butter
2 tablespoons double cream
good wine-glass of Pineau
bouquet garni
pepper

Brown shallots lightly in butter. Add *bouquet garni*, pepper, Pineau, then the mussels. Cover pan, cook gently for 15 minutes. Remove *bouquet garni*. Add cream, stir and serve.

Truite à la Poitevine (Poitevine trout)

For each person, 1 trout washed
1 dessertspoon olive oil
40g butter
2 tablespoons chopped parsley
1 chopped shallot
crushed clove garlic
1 tablespoon white wine vinegar
salt
pepper

Heat oil with one quarter of the butter and fry fish gently, shaking to avoid sticking (about 4 minutes per side — do not overcook). Remove and keep warm in low oven. Add rest of butter to pan, raise heat a little, cook shallots until golden. Add garlic, salt and pepper. Stir, add parsley, stir again, cook a little, add vinegar and let it boil up. Pour over fish.

Languedoc/Roussillon

Brandade de Morue (creamed salt cod)

1 kg salt cod
½ litre olive oil
½ litre milk
1 kg potatoes
2 cloves garlic
grated nutmeg (optional)
pepper
50g grated cheese

This recipe will serve between 6 to 8 people.

The cod needs to be soaked for 12 hours or more, with water changes. Finely chop or crush the garlic cloves. Cook potatoes and mash to a purée. Drain cod, bring it to boil in milk and garlic, take off heat, cover and leave for 10 minutes. Skin and bone cod, flake it and mix with mashed potatoes into a thick purée. Make oil lukewarm. Add milk, garlic and oil very slowly and gently to cod purée, stirring with a spatula, until it is smooth and creamy, like making a mayonnaise. Add pepper and pinch of nutmeg. Serve on fried bread rubbed with garlic, on toast or place in ovenproof dish, dust with grated cheese, and brown under grill.

Bordeaux, Gascony and Les Landes

Rougets à la Girondine (red mullet)

4 medium or 8 small red mullet
50g butter
1 shallot, finely chopped
1 tablespoon chopped parsley
For sauce: 2 wineglasses dry Bordeaux white
1 tablespoon brandy
½ cup fish stock or water
1 clove garlic
1 onion
2 shallots
1 largish mushroom (preferably cèpe)
25g butter
2 tablespoons olive oil
30g flour
bouquet garni
1 tablespoon tomato purée (optional)
salt
pepper

Make sauce first — heat butter and oil, soften in them gently the garlic, onion, shallots and mushroom (preferably *cèpe*, all finely chopped) with lid on. Remove lid and cook until pale golden. Stir in flour, add wine and brandy gradually, stirring until smooth. Add *bouquet garni*, salt, pepper and simmer for 10 minutes. Add fish stock or water, strain, keep hot.

Scale mullet and clean, leaving liver if possible. Cook chopped shallot in butter until pale golden, slide in mullet and cook and brown for 5 minutes on each side. Put them on a hot plate, add sauce to cooking butter for 2 minutes, shaking pan over low heat. Add tomato purée if you wish. Pour sauce over fish. Sprinkle with chopped parsley and serve.

Pays Basque, Béarn and Pyrénées

Saumon ou Truite Braisé au Jurançon (salmon or pink trout braised in Jurançon wine)

4 salmon steaks
4 tomatoes
150g button mushrooms
20g shallots
40g butter
parsley
¼ bottle dry Jurançon wine
4 tablespoons cream
extra knob of butter
salt
pepper

Clean fish, season with salt and pepper. Chop shallots, slice mushrooms thinly, slice tomatoes. Put fish in braising dish, dot with butter, add shallots, mushrooms and tomato rings. Pour wine over it. Cook in hot oven (200°C, 400°F, Mark 6) for 20 minutes. Take out fish and vegetables, keep hot. Drain cooking liquor, add cream, reduce. Whisk in butter. Put vegetable rings round fish, pour sauce over it, sprinkle with parsley.

Provence, Southern Rhône and Côte d'Azur

Thon à la Chartreuse (fresh tunny)

1 to 1¼kg tunny
4 carrots
2 onions
3 lemons
white wine vinegar
½ litre dry white wine
4 cloves garlic
2 teaspoons tomato paste
1 tablespoon flour
olive oil
herb fennel
bay leaf

A delicious change for those of us who only know it canned.

Soak tunny in vinegar and water. Chop carrots, garlic, onions and peeled lemons in very small dice. Sweat in olive oil, add tomato paste and the flour, then the wine, bay and a few sticks of fennel. Add to fish. Just cover with water. Bring to boil over heat, cover with buttered paper and cook in a moderate oven for 30 minutes.

Franche-Comté (Jura), Savoie, Dauphiné

Truites au Bleu (Blue Trout)

6 fresh mountain trout (around 250g) cleaned
750ml white wine vinegar
3 carrots
3 onions
2 shallots
bouquet garni
a few fresh parsley sprigs
lemon wedges
2 litres water
salt
pepper
butter

Called 'Blue Trout' as vinegar turns the skin blueish.

Peel carrots, onions, shallots, cut in thin strips, put in saucepan with the water, *bouquet garni*, parsley sprigs, salt and pepper. Bring to boil. Cover, simmer over low heat 30 minutes. Strain into fish kettle or large pan and leave to cool. Put trout in shallow dish, boil wine vinegar and pour over trout. Leave to cool a little, then plunge the fish into the stock in the fish kettle. Heat slowly until liquid simmers (do not boil). Simmer gently for 20 minutes. Take out trout carefully, sprinkle with chopped parsley. Serve with lemon wedges and hot melted butter.

Alsace and Lorraine

Sandre au Riesling (pike-perch in Riesling wine)

1kg fillets of sandre
4 chopped shallots
chives (if possible)
½ litre of double cream
yolk of egg
1 wine glass of Riesling
same amount of clear fish stock or water

Ask the fishmonger to clean *vider* and fillet the fish, then cut them vertically into thick slices; butter flameproof dish, cover bottom with shallots and chopped chives, put fish slices on it, pour over wine and stock or water and poach until fish is cooked. Remove fish to ovenproof dish, reduce sauce and thicken over low flame with cream, stir in beaten egg yolk. Pour sauce over fish and put in oven to turn light golden. Serve with freshly-cooked noodles.

MAIN COURSES

Normandy

Faisan à la Normande

Brace of pheasant
1½kg cooking apples
½kg dessert apples, (preferably green)
¼ litre double and soured cream mixed
salt
pepper

Any game birds, or duck, can be used as an alternative to pheasant.

Turn pheasants in butter until golden all over. Put in fairly-tight casserole. Peel, core and quarter apples and turn in butter until well covered. Pack apples round the pheasants, season with salt and pepper. Cook in moderate oven (190°C, 375°F, Mark 5) for 50 to 60 minutes. Whisk cream and Calvados and stir gently into apple mixture. Return to oven uncovered for 5 minutes.

Poulet Vallée d'Auge

1 fresh chicken
chopped onion
200g mushrooms sliced thinly
½ bay leaf
sprig of thyme
butter
300ml thick cream
4 tablespoons of Calvados
salt
pepper
herbs

Cut good sized, plump fresh chicken into 6 pieces. Slice white button mushrooms thinly.

Fry chicken pieces in butter, adding salt and pepper as you turn them, for about 15 minutes. Add onion and herbs, flambé the chicken in Calvados, basting, add 4 tablespoons of water, cover and simmer, turning occasionally, for 15 minutes or until nearly cooked. Add mushrooms. Simmer for 10 minutes. Put chicken on very hot dish, add cream to juices and reduce quickly. Pour over chicken.

Picardy and the North

Carbonnade de Boeuf à la Flamande (beef in beer)

750g of lean beef (skirt or chuck)
250g sliced onions
600ml of beer
3 tablespoons of roux (125g each of butter and flour)
lard
3 tablespoons beef stock
1 tablespoon brown sugar
bouquet garni
2 cloves crushed garlic

In Flanders this is served with onions, turnips, carrots and potatoes, not mushrooms and tomatoes, as for most beef cooked in wine.

Cut beef into thick strips 1½cm × 10cm × 5cm. Season them and brown both sides in lard; remove beef; fry onions in same fat. Put beef and onions in casserole in layers with *bouquet garni* and garlic. Dilute pan juices with beer and stock, thicken with roux, add sugar, stir for some minutes, strain into casserole. Bring to boil, cover with lid and cook in moderate oven (160°C, 325°F, Mark 3) for about 2½ hours.

Tourte de Poulet Picarde (Picardy chicken pie)

Chicken (about 1.5kg)
2 sticks celery
large onion
10 leeks
20g fresh cream
125g pickled or smoked tongue (or back bacon)
bouquet garni
flaky pastry
parsley
salt
pepper

Cook chicken in a little water with onion, celery, salt and *bouquet garni* on low heat for 45 minutes. Remove, strain the liquid. Cut leeks into pieces and cook them in a little of the liquid and drain. Skin chicken, cut into pieces and bone. Cut tongue into strips. Place layer of leeks in round oven-proof dish, then chicken, tongue (or bacon), then remaining leeks. Sprinkle generously with parsley. Cover with flaky pastry, with central hole. Bake in oven (240°, 450°F, Mark 8). Heat cream with little salt and pepper. When pie is cooked, pour in cream through hole in centre.

Brittany

Bardatte (stuffed cabbage)

1 cabbage, with good heart
800g boned rabbit (or chicken)
large clove garlic
bunch chervil *or parsley*
300g crustless bread
100ml of milk
100g carrots
100g onions
150 to 200g thin bacon rashers
1 egg
30g chopped shallots
¼ litre Muscadet wine
cooking oil

Soak bread in milk. Separate cabbage leaves, blanch. Chop rabbit meat, shallots, garlic, parsley, mix with bread and egg. Season. Wrap this stuffing in outer cabbage leaves like little parcels, then wrap each parcel in a bacon rasher. Sweat the rest of the cabbage (sliced, unless very small) and onions (sliced) in a little cooking oil and remove to use as garnish. Add Muscadet to pan juices. Add parcels. Cook in oven (200°C, 400°F, Mark 6) for 35 minutes.

La Potée Bretonne (Breton hotpot)

1¼kg shin of beef
750g salted belly of pork
750g bacon
small-medium boiling fowl
250g smoked sausage
250g meat sausage
carrots
turnips
swede
onions
2 large cloves garlic
broad beans
heads of green cabbage
leeks
bouquet garni
salt
pepper

Takes over two hours. Boil shin of beef and chicken in very large pan; skim. Add carrots, turnips, swede cut into large pieces, leeks sliced large, onions whole, bouquet garni. Cook gently for 60 minutes. Add pork, bacon, sausages, garlic, broad beans. Simmer for another hour. Blanch cabbage heads whole for 10 minutes. Drain, add to pot. Season with salt and pepper. Serve with boiled potatoes. Originally cooked over a wood fire with potatoes cooked in the ashes.

Paris and Île de France

Terrine de Gibier (game terrine)

350g greenback streaky bacon rashers
500g game meat off the bone
500g uncooked pork, half fat, half lean, minced
250g diced uncooked ham, half fat
3 tablespoons brandy
3 tablespoons Madeira
½ glass white wine
pinch nutmeg
chopped parsley
chopped ¼ clove garlic
sprinkling of powdered herbs (tarragon, basil, but nothing strong)
pinch allspice (not essential)
salt
black pepper
1 egg

Slice half game meat into finger-size strips (if a game bird, use breast for this). Marinade it with diced ham in Madeira, brandy, wine, herbs, spices and salt and pepper — at least 2 hours, preferably up to 6 hours. Put the rest of the game meat through fine plate of a mincer with minced pork and one bacon rasher. Pour in liquid and herbs from drained marinade, beat in egg and season well.

Line a 1½ litre terrine with bacon slices. Spread a quarter of the stuffing in the terrine, add layer of a third of the game strips and diced ham, cover with another layer of stuffing. Finish layers with stuffing and top with bacon rashers. Put on lid. Put in a roasting dish filled up with water, bring to boil, then put in a hot oven for 1½ hours. Serve cold with crispy bread. Preferably leave up to 3 days in fridge before eating. Will keep a week in a fridge.

Champagne

Andouillettes de Troyes en Feuilletage, et sauce Diable (pork chitterling sausages in flaky pastry with Devil's Sauce)

6 to 8 large andouillettes de Troyes
2 large onions thinly sliced
flaky pastry
4 shallots finely chopped
½ litre dry white wine
200ml wine vinegar
pepper
1 large ladleful of brown sauce or beef stock
parsley chopped

Cook *andouillettes* in hot oven for 20 minutes, then brown

under grill. Set aside. Cook onions in butter until soft. Roll out flaky pastry (enough to encase the sausages) and cut into strips wide enough to take an *andouillette*. Place spoonful of onions on each strip. Wrap up *andouillettes* and cover with pastry lid. Cook in oven for 25 minutes. Serve hot with the sauce.

For sauce: put shallots in a pan with salt and pepper, wine and vinegar. Reduce to a mush, add brown sauce or stock with 1 tablespoon of butter, beating until the mixture boils. Open the cooked *andouillette* cases, pour in a little sauce and cover again. Serve the rest of the sauce, with parsley added, with the *andouillette*.

Cassolette de Ris de Veau à la Champenoise (veal sweetbread casserole)

1.5kg veal sweetbreads
2 onions
3 shallots
100g carrots
100g morilles *for garnish*
½ bottle Coteaux Champagne (still white wine)
400ml fresh cream
salt
pepper
butter
oil

(*Morilles* are often called 'morels' in Champagne and elsewhere. If fresh — in spring — simmer them in butter. You can buy dried *morilles*. Just scald them in boiling water. Or use *cèpes* or small mushrooms simmered in butter.)

Soak sweetbreads, blanch, cool, drain, remove skin carefully. Season. Braise them in the oven on a bed of chopped onions, thinly sliced carrots and shallots in butter and a little oil. Cook in hot oven for 25 minutes. Prepare a light roux with equal quantities of flour and butter. Remove sweetbreads from oven and keep hot. Strain dish juices, skim off as much fat as possible, mix with the roux into smooth sauce. Season.

Slice sweetbreads, put in small casserole with *morilles*, add cream to the sauce, pour sauce over the sweetbreads, simmer for a few minutes and serve.

Pieds de Porc Sainte-Menehould (pigs trotters Saint-Menehould)

Pig's feet
sliced carrot
large onion
bouquet garni

salt
pepper
melted butter
breadcrumbs

You can buy the pig's feet already prepared but not boned, at a boucherie or charcuterie. Tie feet together in pairs and cook in water with carrot, onion, herbs and seasoning. Cook so gently that they are only just boiling. This makes them soft enough to be crunched. Drain, brush them with melted butter, coat with white breadcrumbs, sprinkle with more melted butter and cook in oven until brown. Serve with mashed potatoes.

Loire and Western Loire

Noisettes de Porc aux Pruneaux (nut of meat from pork chump chops with prunes)

4 big pork chops (or one per person)
16 large or 20 smaller prunes
1 finely chopped onion
200ml white wine (Vouvray) or red wine
200ml double cream
40g butter
flour for dusting
1 tablespoon redcurrant jelly (or cranberry)
salt
pepper

This is a simple recipe. Alternatively use the chop on the bone trimmed of fat. We prefer white wine.

Soak prunes overnight in the wine. Dust chops with salt, pepper and flour. Melt butter in largish pan with lid, brown chops on both sides. Tip in prunes and their wine liquid, onion and wine vinegar; cover the pan and simmer for about 50 to 60 minutes. Remove chops to hot dish, surround with prunes. Reduce pan juices, stirring in redcurrant jelly until it dissolves, add cream slowly, let it bubble but stir briskly until smooth. Pour it over the chops.

Burgundy

Boeuf à la Bourguignonne (beef in red wine)

1½kg beef
2 large chopped onions
parsley
thyme
peppercorns
bay leaf
chopped carrot
2 wine glasses of brandy
1 bottle red Burgundy wine
1 tablespoon beef dripping
1½ tablespoons flour
2 cloves crushed garlic

salt and pepper
175g streaky bacon
12 baby onions
250g button mushrooms

This recipe will serve 6 people. The beef should preferably be rolled rump; if not, boned and rolled topside or sirloin. Marinade the beef in brandy (traditional old recipe), turning occasionally, for 6 hours. Or use the wine for marinade. Remove meat and herbs, etc, and drain. Lard meat (or wrap in 2 rashers of the bacon).

Melt dripping in a pan and fry bacon (chopped) and onions gently, then remove. Brown meat well on all sides in same pan; stir in the flour and cook for a minute. Put in casserole. Pour on the marinade (if brandy was used, now add the bottle of red Burgundy wine). Bring to the boil. Add bay, thyme and carrots from marinade, salt and pepper to taste. Cover and cook in preheated moderate oven (160°C, 325°F, Mark 3) for 1½ to 2 hours. Chop the mushrooms in half. Put in bacon, onions and mushrooms. Cook for another hour. Some old recipes add a calf's foot during cooking. Another adds finely sliced oxtail.

Coq au Vin (chicken in wine)

1¼kg chicken or capon
chicken liver
12 button onions
200g button mushrooms, quartered
60g butter
30g flour
2 big cloves garlic
bouquet garni
125g diced streaky bacon
1 bottle red Burgundy
4 tablespoons of marc
salt
pepper
for thickening, 3 tablespoons of chicken or pig's blood or 30g of butter kneaded with flour

The chicken or capon needs to be young and tender. Cut into 6 pieces. Brown the bacon and onions in half the butter. Quarter the mushrooms and separately sauté them in butter. Remove bacon and onions, brown chicken in same pan; sprinkle with flour and let it brown. Put chicken and juices into large casserole, add crushed garlic and wine, bring to boil. Add mushrooms, onions, bacon, marc, *bouquet garni*, seasoning. Cover and simmer 45 to 50 minutes. Put chicken pieces and garniture on hot dish, strain the sauce into a saucepan on low heat. Sauté diced liver fast in butter, liquidise them with the blood or kneaded butter and some marc. Pour simmering sauce slowly into this purée, then pour it over the chicken pieces and garniture.

Gougère (cheese choux pastry)

300ml milk
100g butter
1 teaspoon salt
200g plain flour
4 eggs
150g grated Comté or gruyère cheese

Boil milk with butter and salt. Take off heat, stir in flour; cook stirring over heat. Take off heat, add eggs one at a time to make smooth paste. Stir in 100g cheese and a pinch of white pepper. Pipe into buttered oven dish in a ring, smoothing the sides with a spoon. Brush with beaten egg or milk, sprinkle with rest of cheese. Bake in oven (190°C, 375°F, Mark 5) for 45 minutes until risen and golden. Light meal or starter.

Oeufs en Meurette (poached eggs in red wine)

8 eggs
1 litre of red wine
1 tablespoon chopped shallots
small bouquet garni
very little salt
pepper
50g butter kneaded with 50g flour

Add shallots, herbs and seasoning to wine and boil down by a half. Strain. Over gentle heat poach eggs in it. Put them on hot plate. Thicken wine liquid with kneaded butter, melting it slowly; don't stir. Simmer for a little while. Serve eggs on garlic toast with small sautéed onions and bacon strips. Pour wine sauce over them. Light meal or starter.

Poussin à la Moutarde (small chicken in mustard sauce)

400 to 500g chicken
125g double cream
3 to 4 tablespoons Dijon mustard
salt
pepper
nut of butter

Cover trussed chicken all over with thick layer of mustard. Preheat oven to (220°C, 425°F, Mark 7). Cook chicken until golden brown (about 20 minutes on each side). Heat cream in small pan and pour it over chicken. Cook for another 10 minutes. Put chicken on a hot dish, whisk the sauce and add the butter just before serving. With more cream and mustard and longer cooking, this can succeed with a good tender free range chicken up to 1kg. Split it in two.

Rhône (Lyonnais, Ardèche, Bresse, North Rhône Valley)

Courgettes en Cocottes (courgette moulds with herbs)

1 kg young courgettes
100ml olive oil
70g bread
4 eggs
70g grated gruyère
200g medium-diced onions
3 cloves garlic
6 leaves mint
2 sprigs basil
milk

This recipe will serve up to 8 people. If you have not got eight small ovenproof moulds, use one bigger one. Cut courgettes into large cubes, do not peel; cook with onions, garlic, in olive oil. Soak bread in milk. Drain courgettes, squeeze milk from bread. Add bread, eggs, gruyère, mint, basil to courgettes, season and liquidise. Butter moulds, fill with mixture to cook in *bain-marie* for 30 minutes in slow oven (180°C, 350°F, Mark 4). Turn out and serve hot.

Criques Ardèchoises (grated potato cake)

1 kg potatoes
3 cloves garlic
parsley
oil
3 eggs
flour
salt
pepper

Peel potatoes, grate them, add cloves of garlic and some parsley. Add beaten eggs, a little flour, salt and pepper. Fry mixture in hot oil, in small amounts, to get desired thickness. Turn and fry on other side. Light meal or vegetable dish.

Flan au Foie de Volaille (chicken liver mould)

250g chicken livers
250g cèpes or button mushrooms
3 eggs, plus 2 yolks
½ litre milk
a little butter
parsley

This recipe was given to Arthur years ago by Albert Mazet, chef-patron of Hotel de l'Europe, Vals-les-Bains.

Mince livers with a little parsley, mix with more chopped parsley. Brown them, heat milk and add it. Bring to the boil, allow to cool. Pour mixture onto beaten eggs, season, mix. Pour into buttered mould (or six small moulds). Cook for 20 minutes in a *bain-marie* in slow oven (180°C, 350°F, Mark 4). Sauté *cèpes* or mushrooms. Turn out mould onto hot plate, surround with *cèpes*, pour over it a suitable sauce, preferably tomato.

Poularde à la Nantua (chicken with crayfish or prawn sauce)

There are many versions of this recipe. Here we give the lazy cook's holiday recipe. Stuff a Bresse chicken with flesh of crayfish tails or peeled prawns, chopped, in very thick cream sauce. Poach slowly in chicken stock or seasoned milk. For sauce: make crayfish (or prawn) purée, dilute with butter and cream. If you can buy crayfish or crevette rose butter from the charcuterie or poissonerie, make sauce by simply melting this in an ordinary Béchamel sauce.

Poulet Céléstine (Bresse chicken with tomatoes, mushrooms)

Bresse chicken
250g small mushrooms
1 medium onion finely sliced
4 large or 6 small tomatoes, peeled, seeded, rough chopped
1 litre dry white wine
¼ litre chicken or veal stock (or milk)
¼ litre cream
glass of good brandy
salt
cayenne pepper
2 tablespoons butter

Sweat onions in butter; cut chicken into 6 portions, brown in butter. Add mushrooms and tomatoes and cook for a very short time. Add stock, wine, cayenne pepper, salt. Cover and stew. Take out chicken pieces and mushrooms. Mix in brandy and cream and reduce gently. You can add 2 egg yolks to thicken.

Poitou-Charentes

Côtelettes de Veau Charentaise (veal cutlets Charentaise)

For each person – trimmed veal chop
60g mushrooms
1 tablespoon chopped parsley
25g butter
garlic clove
sheet of greaseproof paper (or foil)

Chop heads of mushrooms finely, mix with chopped parsley, crushed garlic, salt and pepper. Soften butter, then work them all together into a smooth paste. Spread each side of the chop with this paste, wrap each in lightly-oiled grease-proof paper (or foil) and tie tightly. Cook for 50 to 60 minutes according to size of chop in a moderate oven.

Fas de Poitou (vegetable loaf)

Cabbage (about 1½kg)
1kg spinach
handful of sorrel leaves (oseille) with stalks cut out
12 finely chopped shallots
2 tablespoons each of chopped or powdered thyme and marjoram
6 tablespoons chopped parsley
300kg streaky bacon sliced very thinly crosswise
6 eggs
4 cloves garlic
150ml double cream
knob of butter
50g fresh breadcrumbs

Blanch 8 outer leaves of cabbage for 1 minute and keep. Remove core and shred cabbage finely; cut out stalks and shred spinach. Melt butter in large saucepan with lid, add shallots, bacon, shredded greens, garlic and herbs. Mix, cover, and keep over very low heat for 10 minutes (vegetables should reduce by a half). Remove lid and keep over heat until liquid almost evaporates. Beat eggs and cream together and stir gradually into the mixture. Add salt and pepper and breadcrumbs and mix well. Line loaf tin with cabbage leaves, add mixture. Put container in *bain-marie* with about 3 to 4cm of water. Bake in oven for 1 to 1½ hours (190°C, 375°F, Mark 5). Turn out of container, let juices drain, serve hot or cold cut into thick slices. Keep in fridge or freezer.

Mojettes à la Crème (creamed haricot beans)

½kg dried haricot beans
1 onion
carrot
celery stalk
100ml olive oil
200g butter
250ml cream
salt

This recipe must be planned ahead.

Use *crème fraîche* (sour and fresh cream blended — buy it ready made as it takes time, or use thick fresh cream). Soak the beans overnight in cold water. Drain and add onion, carrot, celery, cover with fresh water, bring to the boil, then take off heat and stand for 60 minutes. Drain, remove carrot, onion, celery. Melt 50g of butter in the oil, tip in beans and stir well. Cover with water and simmer for 3 to 4 hours, adding salt towards end. When tender, drain them again, stir in the rest of the butter and cream, put in oven to heat through for about 5 to 10 minutes.

Rognons Flambés au Cognac (kidneys flamed in brandy)

For each person – 3 kidneys of veal
6 to 8 shallots or tiny onions, peeled and blanched in boiling water
6 to 8 small mushrooms, quartered
1 tablespoon butter
lard
sprinkling of flour
150ml dry white wine
2 tablespoons Cognac

The 3 kidneys of veal are preferable but if not available use 4 of lamb. Skin the kidneys, halve them and remove cores. Simmer shallots gently in wine in small covered pan; in a separate pan soften mushrooms slightly in butter and add to shallots. Take off heat and put aside. Heat lard in heavy saucepan over high heat, add kidneys and stir until evenly brown. Flame them with Cognac, sprinkle with flour, season, stir for 3 minutes, then add shallots and mushrooms with liquid. Serve with rice or creamed potatoes.

Périgord, Quercy and Rouergue

Mique Salardaise (dumpling for boiling bacon or salt pork)

1kg salt pork or bacon
1 large boiling sausage
carrots
celery
leek
turnips
cabbage
300g stale bread cubes
salt
3 eggs
1 tablespoon pork fat

This recipe will serve 6 people.

Simmer pork in water for 2 hours, add sausage and vegetables. Meanwhile make dumplings by working bread, eggs, pork fat with salt into a dough, rolling into a ball and dusting with flour. Lower into pot with meat and vegetables, cook for 15 minutes on each side.

Poule au Pot (rustic chicken stew)

Chicken
2 tablespoons goose fat (or pork dripping)
1 large onion, chopped
100g breadcrumbs
1 clove garlic
4 egg yolks
500g each of carrots, leeks, turnips and Swiss chard (blette – *leaves of white beet)*
bouquet garni
1 onion, preferably stuck with 3 or 4 cloves

This is the recipe which made Henry IV say that every French family should have one each week – takes 3 hours simmering. Use a large boiling fowl (not a young chicken or frozen chicken) with giblets and chicken's blood (if the boucherie will give it to you). Use milk if you cannot get blood.

Soak bread in chicken's blood, add finely chopped liver, heart and gizzard, chopped onion and garlic. Bind with egg yolks, season and stuff chicken with this mixture. Brown chicken on all sides in fat. Cover with boiling salted water and leave to simmer gently (3 hours for big boiling fowl). Vegetables, cleaned and trimmed should be added for last hour. Serve hot. Locally, the chicken is often served with a thick green sauce (*sauce verte*) which can be made two ways: by adding mayonnaise to a purée of green herbs (spinach, watercress, parsley, chervil, chives, perhaps tarragon) or by mixing oil and vinegar with finely chopped shallot, chives, parsley, and yolk of hard boiled egg.

Massif Central (Limousin, Auvergne, Bourbonnais)

Médaillons de Veau au Citron (veal medallions in lemon)

4 medaillons *(small rounds) veal about 120g each*
200ml dry white wine
300ml single cream
2 lemons
1 orange
2 leeks
200g carrots
200g turnips
butter

Cook veal until brown in butter. Take out veal and keep hot. Steam carrots, leeks and turnips separately. Pour white wine and juice from lemons and orange into pan of butter and meat juices, reduce, then add cream. Cut lemon and orange rind without pith into *julienne* (matchstick) strips and blanch, then add them to the sauce. Pour sauce over meat and vegetables.

Potée Auvergnate (Auvergne hotpot)

2 firm-hearted cabbages (about 250g each) cut into quarters
knuckle of ham
bacon joint (500 to 750g) blanched
1 kg turnips, quartered
500g leeks
1 kg carrots
4 medium-sized whole onions
1 kg medium-sized whole potatoes
white stock, water or mixture
1 large or 2 to 3 smaller cervelas *(saveloy-type raw sausage)*

To serve 6 people.

Cover meat and all vegetables except potatoes with water or stock, season, simmer, covered, for 1½ to 2 hours. Add potatoes and sausage, cook for 30 minutes or until potatoes are done. Drain before serving. Save stock for another meal (i.e. cooking cabbage in strips for 10 minutes).

Poulet au Fromage (chicken in cheese)

Free-range or good boiling fowl (around 2 kg)
1 bottle of dry white wine
large carrot
large onion
2 largish leeks
bouquet garni
cloves
peppercorns
garlic clove
1 litre of good chicken stock if possible
2 egg yolks
50g butter
2 tablespoons flour
200 ml cream
cupful of grated cheese, preferably mixed gruyère and local fourme d'Ambert or tomme

Poach fowl until tender in stock (or water) and wine, with vegetables, herbs and seasoning. Strain stock. Melt butter in a saucepan, add flour and stir over heat to make a roux, then stir in enough of the chicken stock to make a thick, smooth sauce. Let it cool a little, then thicken with egg yolks and cream. Cut chicken into pieces and coat each piece thoroughly with sauce. Sprinkle liberally with cheese. Brown under grill.

Languedoc/Roussillon

Cassoulet de Toulouse

700g dry white beans (soaked for 4 hours plus)
2 litres water
300g salt pork and 300g salt bacon, both soaked overnight
*200g fresh pork rind (*cuennes de porc*)*
2 peeled carrots
4 garlic cloves, chopped
bouquet garni
1 whole onion, 2 chopped
2 tablespoons goose fat
boned shoulder of lamb, cut in chunks
about 20cm of Toulouse sausage, sliced thickly
8 to 10 thick slices of garlic sausage
2 pieces of confit *of goose or duck (400 to 500g)*
1 cup of breadcrumbs
salt
pepper

Will serve 8 people.

Simmer beans in water with pork, ham, pork rind tied in bundle, 2 carrots, whole onion, 2 garlic cloves, *bouquet garni*, until beans are tender but not breaking up – about 1½ hours. Sauté lamb in goose fat until chunks are brown all over. Add chopped onions, 2 garlic cloves and cook until golden. Just cover meat with bean pot liquid. Add salt and pepper. Cover. Simmer very slowly for 1½ hours. Brown Toulouse sausage in fat, add this and garlic sausage to meat and simmer another 15 minutes. Discard *bouquet garni*, whole carrots and onion. Cut meat and rind from both pots into big pieces. Put half the beans in the bottom of a big, ovenproof pot, preferably earthenware, add all the meat, including *confit*, enough juices from pots to keep moist. Top with rest of beans, bring to boil, sprinkle with breadcrumbs. Put in a preheated moderate oven (165°-175°C, 320°-350°F, Mark 1). Bake for about 2 hours, breaking crust as it forms, stirring, then sprinkling more breadcrumbs. Leave last crust to brown. In a very low oven, it can just simmer for hours.

Épaule de Mouton en Pistache (shoulder of mutton Catalan-style)

Shoulder of mutton (buy ready boned, rolled and tied)
large slice of unsmoked raw ham
sliced onion and carrot
*2 tablespoons goose fat (*graisse d'oie*)*
2 tablespoons flour
400ml clear soup or brown stock
¼ litre white wine

50 blanched cloves of garlic (10 will do!)
bouquet garni

Line a saucepan with ham, onion and carrot. Put in rolled mutton, pour over it melted goose fat (or lard). Season, cover, cook very gently for 30 minutes. Take mutton and ham out of saucepan. Put in flour and brown it. Moisten with white wine, add soup or stock. Mix well, strain. Dice ham, put back in saucepan with mutton. Add blanched garlic cloves, *bouquet garni* and a piece of dried orange peel (optional). Moisten with the strained stock. Cover, cook in moderate oven for about 60 minutes. Drain and untie shoulder. Put it on a serving dish. Pour over it the sauce and garlic.

Bordeaux, Gascony and Les Landes

Carbonnade Gasconne (traditional braised veal)

1.2kg veal rump
500g sausage meat
4 shallots
3 cloves garlic
bunch parsley
2 tablespoons olive oil
1 lemon
breadcrumbs

Enough for 8 people or two meals.

Preheat oven (to 220°C, 425°F, Mark 7). Put veal, in 3 to 4cm thick slices, in large casserole in a little olive oil. Chop shallots, garlic and parsley. Mix sausage meat with garlic, shallots and parsley, salt and pepper and spread in an even layer over the meat, pressing down with your hands. Sprinkle more olive oil, cook uncovered in oven for 60 minutes. Cover loosely with foil if sausage gets too brown. Some 10 minutes before end of cooking, sprinkle breadcrumbs mixed with juice of lemon and baste with meat juices. Freshly cooked young vegetables and *cèpes à la Bordelaise* go well with it.

Chou Rouge Landais (red cabbage with sausage)

1 to 1½kg red cabbage
large cooking apple
1 to 1½kg large garlicky raw sausage or boiling ring
½kg onions
1 large green pepper
2 tablespoons olive oil
2 tablespoons wine vinegar
100ml red wine
50g brown sugar
2 to 4 cloves garlic, to taste
salt
pepper
chopped parsley
pinch each of cinnamon and mustard powder

Plan ahead as this recipe takes about 2¾ hours.

Shred cabbage finely, discarding core and outer leaves. Peel and chop onions and apple. Deseed and chop the pepper. Put them all in ovenproof dish with close-fitting lid. Add crushed garlic, oil, sugar, salt, pepper and other seasonings, vinegar, but not wine. Cover, shake well. Cook in moderate oven (170°C, 350°F, Mark 3) for 40 minutes. Stir, bury sausage in the middle, add wine, cook for another 2 hours.

Pays Basque, Béarn and the Pyrénées

Garbure

2 litres water
can (4 portions) confit d'oie *(goose) or* confit de canard *(duck)*
250g belly of pork or uncooked bacon
150g dried or 200g fresh haricot beans
400g potatoes
1 small green cabbage
1 large leek
4 carrots
1 turnip
2 cloves garlic
4 thin slices of rough country bread

If using dried beans soak overnight. Peel and clean vegetables, cut in large pieces. Remove leaves of cabbage, cut out stalk and cut leaves into very thin strips. Boil water, add vegetables, pork cut into large pieces and garlic, season, boil for 60 minutes. Add goose or duck *confit*, leaving fat around one portion. Cook 15 minutes. Put bread in each bowl with portion of *confit* on it, then vegetables and broth.

Poulet Basque (Basque chicken)

Roasting chicken, about 2kg
cayenne pepper
salt
parsley
2 to 3 green and 2 to 3 red peppers, deseeded and sliced coarsely
100g mushrooms (halved or quartered)
5 tomatoes, skinned, quartered, deseeded
125g lean smoked bacon
1 tiny chilli, deseeded and chopped very fine
1 clove garlic
100ml white wine
goose or pork fat (in jars from boucherie)

Cut chicken into serving pieces and dust with flour, brown gently in the fat for about 15 minutes. Add bacon cut in small pieces, the chilli and peppers, tomatoes, mushrooms. Mix with wooden spoon until all begin to cook.

Add garlic, salt, cayenne pepper and pour on the wine. Cover and cook for about 20 minutes. Serve topped with parsley, surrounded by boiled rice.

Provence, Southern Rhône and the Côte d'Azur

Boeuf en Daube (beef casseroled in Provence way)

1½kg chuck steak or shin of beef
150g lean streaky green bacon, cut into strips
2 tablespoons olive oil
2 shallots chopped
For marinade: 1 litre red wine
2 sliced onions
wine glass of wine vinegar
3 finely sliced carrots
4 cloves garlic crushed
bouquet garni *containing strip of orange peel*
parsley stems
bay leaf
stick of celery
8 black peppercorns
savory
oregano
thyme
marjoram (or mixed dried Provençal herbs)
2 crushed juniper berries (optional)

The old *daubière* was a stone or earthenware casserole.

Remove all fat from beef, cut into cubes and marinade them overnight. Remove pieces from marinade to dry about 4 to 5 hours before you intend to eat the stew. In a large casserole, heat olive oil and sauté bacon and shallots. Add pieces of beef and let them brown all over. Add well-drained vegetables from marinade. While stirring, let them brown a little, then add *bouquet garni*, and marinade liquid including peppercorns. If the meat is not quite covered, top up with more wine. Season well. Heat oven (to 200°C, 400°F, Mark 6). Cover tightly, using oiled greaseproof paper if necessary under lid, bring to boil, put in oven and cook for 3 hours or more. Serve with mixture of several seasonal vegetables.

Tian de Courgettes et de Tomates (courgette and tomato flan)

1kg tomatoes
1kg courgettes
2 sliced onions
1 red, 1 green pepper, seeded and cut in rounds
2 aubergines, thinly sliced
1 large clove garlic, sliced
6 tablespoons olive oil
50g grated Parmesan cheese
5 pinches savory and thyme

Use ovenproof flan dish for cooking. Heat half olive oil in frying pan, fry onions golden, add peppers, aubergines and garlic, season, cook gently, stirring occasionally. Slice courgettes and tomatoes into rounds. Put softened peppers, aubergines and onions into bottom of dish. Arrange courgettes and tomatoes on top in overlapping rows. Sprinkle with thyme, savory, seasoning and olive oil. Bake for 45 minutes (at 180°C, 350°F, Mark 4), then 15 minutes before the end, sprinkle with Parmesan and rest of olive oil.

Tourte de Canard (duck pie)

400g flaky pastry
½kg duck meat off bone
300g lean veal
300g neck of pork
Marinade: glass of Cognac
2 sliced onions
2 sliced shallots
salt
pepper
thyme
bay leaf
parsley
1 bottle of white wine

Overnight marinade.

Chop meat into fairly large chunks and marinade overnight. Make pastry. Line pie dish with pastry, add marinaded meat still wet, salt, pepper. Cover with fine layer of flaky pastry. Make small hole in top. Cook in oven (at 200°C, 400°F, Mark 6) for 30 minutes.

Franche-Comté (Jura), Savoie and Dauphiné

Escalope de Veau Jurassienne à la Compote d'Oignons (Jura veal escalopes with onions)

4 escalopes (about 200-225g each)
200g Comté gruyère cheese
4 slices of cured, raw ham
2 eggs
breadcrumbs
oil
butter
15g truffles
For onion compote: 400g onions finely sliced
150ml wine vinegar
75ml thick cream
60g butter

Flatten the escalopes with the side of a heavy blade to break fibres. Slice in half horizontally, leaving halves attached at end. Put in the escalope 'sandwich' a slice of cured ham, a thin slice of cheese and thin strips of truffle. You can buy truffles canned but they are pricey – if too dear, use *morilles*, *cèpes* or even buttom mushrooms. Beat together eggs, ½ tablespoon of oil and salt. Dip escalopes in this, then cover both sides with breadcrumbs. Season. Heat oil and butter in a pan and cook escalopes for about 5 minutes on each side until cooked.

Heat butter in a fresh pan, soften onions in it. Add vinegar, salt and pepper and simmer slowly until onions are really soft and mushy. Stir in cream. Serve each escalope on top of a spoonful of stewed onions. Top with lemon slices or creamed spinach.

Gratin Dauphinois (potato gratin)

1 kg firm potatoes
600 ml milk
200 ml thickish cream
75 g butter
2 cloves garlic

Peel, wash and wipe potatoes which should preferably be yellow inside, which makes a difference. When dry, slice thin, put in saucepan and pour on the milk. Add salt, pepper and one crushed garlic clove. Cook on a low flame until all milk has been absorbed (takes time – beware of burning at the end, but do not stir potatoes; try not to break them). Rub a flattish oven dish thoroughly with juice of other garlic clove. Lay potatoes in it. Cover with cream and add butter in small knobs dotted around surface. Cook in slow oven for 1 to 1½ hours, turning up at end to brown potatoes in top. Says the Tourist Board: 'Gratin is like royalty, it dislikes being kept waiting.' Meal or serve with meat.

Pormonniers (Annecy herby sausage)

6 pormonniers *or similar*
1 French large pork sausage
1 kg potatoes
½ bottle of Savoy white wine

Prick pork sausage and simmer with a little salt in a saucepan in the wine and a ½ litre of water for 45 minutes. Prick the *pormonniers* without splitting the skins and put in the pan with pork sausage. Bring back to boiling point and add peeled potatoes cut into large pieces. Simmer until potatoes are cooked.

Alsace and Lorraine

Choucroute Garnie à l'Alsacienne (sauerkraut and sausages)

3kg sauerkraut
½ shoulder of smoked pork (épaule fumée)
500g piece of smoked bacon (lard fumé)
500g salted pork (lard salé)
250g white sausage (saucisse blanche)
8 Montbéliard sausages (sausages with caraway seeds – replaceable by others)
8 small Strasbourg sausages (Wiennerle) *or 4 large Strasbourg or Knackwurst*
2 black puddings (boudins noirs)
200g lard (called saindoux, *not* lard)
1 medium chopped onion
bay leaf
3 cloves (clous de girofle)
4 to 8 juniper berries (baies de genièvre)
3 cloves garlic crushed
½ litre Riesling or Sylvaner wine
¼ litre bouillon *or beef stock*
piece of muslin

You can replace sausages with other smoked ones, but you must include white veal sausages and Strasbourg sausages or some similar knackwurst.

Melt lard in deep saucepan and lightly fry onion. Pour in wine and *bouillon.* Add meats (not sausages) cut into 6 to 8 pieces. Put sauerkraut (canned or from barrel) rinsed in hot water and squeezed dry on top, add seasoning. Wrap cloves, bay leaf, garlic and juniper berries in muslin and put in before putting on lid. Cook on low heat for 1½ hours. Simmer in separate pan Strasbourg and Montbéliard sausages but do not let them boil. Fry white sausage and black puddings. Place sauerkraut and meat on serving dish, pile sausages on and around it, surround with small boiled potatoes.

Gelée de Canard (duck in jelly)

6 good size thighs of duck (or half a duck with bones)
1 pied de veau *(calf's foot)*
6 cloves garlic
2 carrots
3 shallots
bouquet garni
1 litre of Pinot Noir Alsatian rosé wine

You will need to plan ahead; overnight marinade plus 24 hours in fridge.

Marinade joints of duck overnight in vegetables, garlic,

bouquet garni and wine. Dry duck joints and fry in butter until just golden. Put in saucepan. Add calf's foot chopped in 3 and marinade juice, herbs and vegetables; season. Simmer for 2 hours, skimming and removing fat. Take out duck and carrots. Drain liquid, cool in fridge and remove fat. Cut duck meat off bone and dice it. Dice carrots. Put duck and carrot pieces into one large or several small moulds. Warm up defatted juices, pour over the duck (one friend of ours adds a little pure orange juice to the liquid). Put in fridge for 24 hours to jellify. Serve with slices of duck liver pâté and asparagus or whites of young leeks in vinaigrette sauce or cucumber in cream sauce.

Tourte de la Vallée de Munster (Munster Valley pie)

Make puff pastry (Alsatians use ½ butter, ½ lard)
500g lean pork (boneless shoulder) and 300g veal (neck is usual) or 800g pork
2 white bread rolls or equivalent French bread crumbled into milk and soaked
1 small chopped onion
clove of garlic, crushed
2 eggs
½ teaspoon salt
⅛ teaspoon pepper
⅛ teaspoon ground nutmeg

Serve hot with vegetables, cold with salad.

Mince meat, onion, bread, garlic. Add 1 egg and seasoning. Mix thoroughly. Line a pie dish (about 25cm diameter) with pastry, bringing edges well over the lip. Separate second egg, place mixture evenly in dish and brush top with egg white. Cover with pastry, brush top of pie with egg yolk, make small evaporation hole in top. Bake in preheated oven (200°C, 400°F, Mark 6) for 45 minutes.

DESSERTS

Picardy and the North

Flan de Carottes Flamand (sweet carrot flan)

Pastry
butter
custard
carrots
sugar
icing sugar

Line buttered tart tin with pastry. Fill with finely chopped carrots boiled in very little water and mixed with butter, sugar, and several tablespoons of thick custard. Bake in moderate oven. Just before taking it out, sprinkle with icing sugar and leave in to glaze.

Normandy

Omelette Normande

4 cooking apples
wine glass Calvados
butter
6 eggs
3 tablespoons cream
sugar
salt

(This is the sweet version – another is filled with shellfish and cream.)

Peel, core and slice apples thinly. Soften in melted butter, tablespoon of Calvados and a little sugar. When tender, stir, sprinkle with a little more sugar, heat in moderate oven until sugar starts to caramelise. Whisk eggs, cream, salt and make an omelette with rest of butter. Slide it on a hot dish, cover with apple mixture, sprinkle sugar over it and flame with the rest of the Calvados.

Brittany

Crêpes (sweet pancakes)

150g fine sugar
500g fine wheat flour
pinch of salt
8 eggs
300ml cream (not essential)
1 litre milk (or half milk/half water)
80g cooled melted butter

Add sugar, salt, eggs to flour and work smooth. Whisk in gently cream, milk and butter and leave batter to rest for an hour if possible (Bretons often add a tablespoon of rum or Cognac). Lightly oil a large frying pan and heat until it shimmers. Stir batter, pour in a ladleful, tilt pan until bottom is covered. The pancake should be very thin. Turn it almost immediately with a spatula and cook other side. Pile up *crêpes* on hot dish as you cook them. If any get coldish, reheat. You can even deep-freeze them. Spread with jam, honey, strawberries, cream or what you wish and roll.

Champagne

Bombe Glacée au Marc de Champagne

½ litre boiled milk
4 egg yolks
125g sugar
100g glacé cherries

Make an egg custard by beating egg yolks and sugar together in top half of a double pan over low heat. When mixture thickens a little, add milk gradually, stirring again, until mixture thickens. Put in a freezing compartment. Decorate with glacé cherries and pour over it marc de Champagne.

Loire and Western Loire

Crémets d'Angers or de Saumur (cream cheese mixed with fresh cream and egg whites)

250g crémets *(like cottage cheese)*
60g fine sugar
whites of 3 eggs
pinch of salt
100ml thick cream

Served with fruit and cream as dessert or for breakfast.

Drain cheese in a sieve (if necessary). Put in mixing bowl; whisk in cream until smooth and thick; beat in sugar. Whip egg whites with salt until stiff, fold into mixture. Tip onto square of muslin, pull corners together, tie and hang in fridge with bowl to catch drips. It should stay there 24 hours. Serve with cream and fruit.

Pithiviers (almond cake)

500g puff pastry
100g ground almonds
125g fine sugar
50g butter
2 whole eggs, plus 1 yolk
1 tablespoon flour
3-4 tablespoons rum

Roll out pastry and cut into two, one piece thicker than the other. Beat almonds, sugar, butter, flour, whole eggs and rum together for 5 to 6 minutes. Spread this filling on the thinner piece of pastry and cover with the other piece. Score top of tart with knife, brush with egg yolk and bake in hot oven for 30 minutes. Preferably serve hot, but it is pleasant cold.

Tarte Tatin (upside-down apple tart)

500g firm apples sliced
short pastry
125g butter
150g sugar
serve with cream

Butter a 27cm tart tin with 2 tablespoons butter, sprinkle with half the sugar. Arrange apple slices in pan, sprinkle with rest of sugar. Dot with rest of butter in small pieces. Put pan over hot heat on top of cooker for about 3 minutes to caramelise the sugar. Cover with pastry. Bake 30 minutes (180°C, 350°F, Mark 4). Turn onto plate with caramelised apples on top.

Rhône (Lyonnais, Ardèche, Bresse, North Rhône Valley)

Flan aux Marrons (chestnut custard)

500g tin of chestnut purée
¼ litre milk
100ml cream
3 eggs
2 tablespoons rum
a pinch of powdered vanilla
tube of caramel

Beat chestnut purée, cream and eggs with a fork in a bowl. Add rum and vanilla. Caramelise a metal mould by using paste as directed or by melting sugar slightly moistened in a little water in the mould until slightly brown, then rotating mould until the caramel coats the interior. Pour in the mixture, cook in a *bain-marie* in hot oven for 45 minutes. Cool in the mould and turn out just before serving, with whipped or Chantilly cream.

Gâteau Lyonnais (Lyonnais cake)

200g butter
200g caster sugar
300g flour
4 eggs
1 teaspoon baking powder
2 ripe pears
¾kg ripe apricots
75g praline*(almond in sugar coating from pâtisserie)*
a little icing sugar (optional)
a few drops of vanilla extract

Serve cold with fresh cream.

Cut butter in pieces, cream with wooden spoon. Beat in sugar, then eggs, one at a time. When smooth and light, work in baking powder, flour and a few drops of vanilla extract.

Peel, quarter and core pears, slice thinly. Halve apricots, remove stones. Coarsely grind *praline* with rolling pin.

Butter and flour 24cm cake tin. Pour in 1½cm of batter. Cover with pear slices. Pour over thin layer of cake batter, add apricots cut side down. Sprinkle with crushed *praline*, cover with rest of batter. Put in oven (preheated to 180°C, 350°F, Mark 4) for 10 minutes. Turn off oven, leave cake in it for 10 minutes more. Remove cake from cake pan, cool, sprinkle with icing sugar. Serve as dessert with fresh cream.

Poitou-Charentes

Parfait au Cognac

2 egg yolks
50g icing sugar
1 to 2 drops vanilla essence according to taste
250ml crème fraîche *bought ready prepared or thick cream*
100ml Cognac

This dessert should be made at least 6 hours before needed.

Put cream in coldest part of refrigerator to make more solid, then whip until fairly thick. Beat egg yolks thoroughly; beat in icing sugar, then vanilla. Mix in Cognac slowly. Fold cream gradually into this mixture. Pour into container and freeze in deep freezer or ice-compartment of refrigerator for 6 hours or more. Can be kept deep-frozen.

Périgord, Quercy and Rouergue

Les Merveilles (pastry fritters)

500g flour
5 eggs
100g butter, softened
1 tablespoon baking powder (not necessary but makes dish lighter)
200g icing sugar
oil for deep frying
flavouring of your choice (juice of lemon or grated rind or tablespoon orange flower water or tablespoon brandy)

Mix flour, baking powder and eggs in bowl with softened butter, salt and flavouring. Work to a smooth dough, roll out to 6mm thick, cut into strips 15cm long by 2cm wide. Fry pastry strips in deep oil. They puff up and brown quickly. Turn once, take out with a slotted spoon, drain, sprinkle with lots of icing sugar. Serve hot or keep in airtight tin for snacks.

Massif Central

Gâteau aux Poires (pear gâteau)

1 kg pears
big wine glass of eau-de-vie *(local version is called* gnôle*)*
100g caster sugar
1 packet vanilla sugar (or 2 tablespoons caster sugar with a few drops of vanilla)
*140g self-raising flour (*farine à levure*) — or use ordinary flour and add a packet of* levure chimique*)*
100ml milk
100ml oil
3 eggs
a little butter

Plenty here for 6 to 8 people.

Peel and core pears, slice thinly and soak in *eau-de-vie*. Make a well in centre of flour; add sugar, vanilla sugar and *levure* if necessary. Pour in milk, oil and eggs. Mix well. Gently fold in pears. Pour into ovenproof mould and cook for an hour in slow oven (160°C, 325°F, Mark 3).

Languedoc/Roussillon

Crème d'Homère (wine and honey cream)

150g clear honey
½ litre sweetish white wine
4 eggs
2 egg yolks
125g sugar
pinch of cinnamon
strip lemon peel
water

Simmer very slowly the wine and honey, with cinnamon and peel. Beat the eggs while liquid cools a little. Pour hot liquid slowly onto beaten eggs, whisking non-stop. To caramelise a large mould, heat sugar with 4 tablespoons of water in a thick-based saucepan, bring to the boil, stirring to melt sugar. Stop stirring and watch until syrup turns just brown. Take it off quickly and pour into mould, tilting until bottom and sides are covered. Pour in the honey mixture and cook in a moderate oven (160°C, 325°C, Mark 3) for 35 minutes. Cool in fridge.

Bordeaux, Gascony and Les Landes

Croustade aux Pruneaux (prune tart)

450g prunes
2 eggs
80ml milk
250g butter
250g flour
grated orange rind
sugar
pinch of salt

This is really much nicer than it sounds!

Soak prunes overnight in white wine. Make pastry by mixing flour, well-beaten eggs, salt and milk, working it well. Roll in ball and leave to rest for 2 hours. Simmer prunes in wine until almost all liquid has gone, cool and stone. Roll out pastry and cover central third of its area with generous slices of butter, using half of it. Fold one end over this central part, cover it with rest of butter, then fold the remaining third over the top. Let it rest for another 30 minutes, then roll out very thinly indeed. Cut a round big enough to line a round tin, cover it with prunes and grate orange rind over them. Put second round of pastry on top, moisten edges and pinch them well together. Prick top layer in a few places, sprinkle sugar over it. Cook in oven (at 190°C, 375°F, Mark 5) for 25 minutes or until pastry is golden. Serve warm.

Provence, Southern Rhône and Côte d'Azur

Tarte aux Epinards (spinach tart)

1kg spinach, stemmed and washed thoroughly
3 eggs
⅓ litre double cream
100g sugar
nutmeg
grated rind of lemon
¼ cup sultanas or currants (optional)
short crust pastry shell, baked blind
salt

Put spinach into large pot of slightly salted boiling water, return to the boil, pushing all spinach underwater. Almost immediately, when spinach is limp, drain it, put it under cold running water, squeeze thoroughly in your hands into a ball. Chop coarsely and put in mixing bowl. In another bowl mix eggs, cream, sugar, grated lemon rind, pinch of salt and grated nutmeg. Add to spinach, add sultanas or currants, mix thoroughly. Pour into pastry shell, bake for 30 minutes (at 190°C, 375°F, Mark 5). Filling should swell and colour lightly. Serve hot or cold as starter or dessert.

Franche-Comté (Jura), Savoie, Dauphiné

Soufflé de Chartreuse (iced Chartreuse soufflé)

8 egg yolks
450g sugar
¾ litre fresh cream
100 to 150ml green Chartreuse liqueur
125ml water

You need a freezer or deep ice tray.

Take a round freezable mould about 18cm and make a collar of greaseproof paper 3cm higher than the edge. Stick ends together with butter and keep in place with string or a rubber band. Oil dish and sprinkle with a little sugar. Boil water and sugar in a saucepan for 10 minutes. Beat eggs, then beat the syrup into them in a thin trickle. Place the bowl over a pan of hot water and continue to beat until mixture sticks to blades of beater. Leave to get cold. Whip the cream and flavour with Chartreuse. Mix this with eggs and syrup. Fill mould to within 1cm of top of paper. Put in freezer section of fridge for at least 4 hours.

Alsace and Lorraine

Tarte aux Quetsches (purple plum tart)

Pastry: 1½ cups flour
¼ cup butter
*¼ cup lard (*saindoux*)*
⅛ teaspoon salt
½ cup water
extra tablespoon butter for greasing tart dish
1½kg Quetsche plums (washed and stoned)
½ cup granulated sugar
¼ teaspoon cinnamon
1 tablespoon instant tapioca

Mix pastry ingredients in bowl, adding water last. Shape into ball, roll out on floured board to fit 25cm buttered tart dish. Line dish. Cut plums in half, put in tart dish skin down. Sprinkle with sugar, cinnamon, then tapioca. Heat oven (to 200°C, 400°F, Mark 6) and bake tart for 40 minutes until crust is golden and plums cooked. Serve with whipped double cream.

Weights and Measures

The following tables are approximate and simplified for easy conversion.

SOLID

Ounces	*Grams*
½	15
1	30
2	60
2½	75
3	90
3½	100
4	120
5	150
6	180
7	210
8	250
9	280
10	300
11	330
12	360
1lb	500
2¼lb	1kg
3lb	1½kg

LIQUID

British Imperial	*Metric*
1fl oz	25ml
2fl oz	50ml
3fl oz	75ml
4fl oz	100ml
5fl oz	125ml
½pt	¼ litre
1pt	½ litre
1¼pt	¾ litre
1¾pt	1 litre

American	*Metric*
1fl oz	30ml
2fl oz	60ml
3fl oz	90ml
4fl oz	120ml
5fl oz	150ml
½pt	¼ litre
1pt	½ litre
1½pts	¾ litre
2pts	1 litre

OVEN TEMPERATURES

	Centigrade	Gas	Fahrenheit
Very cool	130°C	½	250°F
	140°C	1	275°F
Cool	150°C	2	300°F
Warm	170°C	3	325°F
Moderate	180°C	4	350°F
Fairly hot	190°C	5	375°F
	200°C	6	400°F
Hot	220°C	7	425°F
Very hot	230°C	8	450°F
	240°C	9	475°F
	250°C	10	500°F

MEASUREMENTS

0.4 in	1 cm
0.8 in	2 cm
1.2 in	3 cm
1.6 in	4 cm
2 ins	5 cm
2.4 ins	6 cm
2.8 ins	7 cm
3 ins	8 cm
3.5 ins	9 cm

Index